MARKET

of

FRANCE

Janice Gallagher

Loisirs Publications

First published in the United Kingdom 2001
by
Loisirs Publications
Loisirs House
27 Eagle Road
Bishops Green
Newbury
Berkshire RG20 4HP
Telephone: 01635 269139

ISBN 1-903861-00-4

for my children

Anthony, Neil, Gareth

and

Emily - Rose

with a special thanks to

Neil

Photographs

Alan John Gallagher

Table of Contents

Introduction

When I first started travelling to France many, many years ago, I thought that markets were places to make the francs go a little bit further. Nothing was further from the truth. I was amazed to find that almost without exception the quality on offer in the markets was far superior to anything that I had hitherto experienced. Very often, the produce will be more expensive than the local supermarket. When you take into account the work that goes into producing much of this food, the freshness of the product and the quality, is it any wonder that the French would rather shop at a local market and regularly do so. Since then, markets have been my passion and finding each new one has been just as exciting as the first and if I am honest, one of the chief reasons I fell in love with France so long ago.

My husband tells me I can smell a market at twenty miles. I can ! A mere glimpse of a gaily coloured piece of canvas prompts me to reach for the map to find the next exit off the autoroute or pore over town maps to find the first turning off. This usually turns out to be a complicated one way system and has us driving around for hours with me becoming more and more determined by the minute to find that seductive piece of tent. Very often that is exactly what it has turned out to be. A Tent! This is how we have found otherwise unknown campsites but that's another story.

The only times I have actually managed to arrive at a market early, is when we disembark from the ultra early ferry from Portsmouth and then we even get there before the stallholders! One of my favourites haunts is Honfleur on a bright summer's morning. The shops are all closed, the streets are deserted, parking is possible and the architecture is spellbinding. You can almost taste the sea and I eagerly anticipate the fisherman's catch on sale, later in the morning.

When I find one of these little gems it is invariably later in the morning than usual and fearing that the owners are at any minute going to start dismantling this cornucopia of delights, I rush round like a puppy in a new house for the very first time. Satisfied that I have explored everything, smelt all of the new smells and finding my curiosity satisfied, I then get down to the real business in hand. The second advance. In a matter of minutes I have planned and charted my course with meticulous precision. Slower and more sedately this time, I set off to find all of those things I could not possibly do without or my holiday would be ruined. Emerging later with a state of the art, all singing , all dancing, glass lidded frying pan, I sniff the air to locate the smell of fresh coffee. Finding a bar, we sit with our delicious cup of real coffee and contentedly reminisce over the events of the morning.

The enticing smell of spit roasting chicken, hissing " buy me! buy me!" spinning away above a tray of tiny, perfectly round white potatoes luxuriating in a bath of spices and meat juices. The glistening bowls of olives, stuffed with delicious delicasies of every colour and fragrance imaginable. Mounds of cheeses lovingly made by their dedicated owners who are gently imitating the sound of a sheep, for a shopper unfamiliar with the language. Hoops and hoops of sausages, strands of pink and white garlic looking for all the world like a bride's bouqet. Small delicately perfumed melons squeezed and sniffed by a knowledgeable Madame intent on her familiy's next repast. A hillock of fresh fish, artfully arranged to tempt even the most ambivalent of fish eaters to sample their wares. Frilly lettuces, posies of radishes and acre after acre of luscious red juicy tomatos. Some of the stalls may only consist of a few odd shaped, unwashed vegetables or a few mis-shapen apples or pears, maybe even a bunch of brilliant dahlias. These are the growers who have picked them fresh from their gardens that morning and will be the freshest produce you have ever had. Unless of course you already grow your own, when you will appreciate the labour of love that goes into them.

No visit to a market is complete without those little snacks to fortify you as you begin the task of improving the stallholders financial standing. The croissants, freshly baked just a short time ago, that crumble all down your front at the first bite (they just are not the same from the supermarkets where they have been made days before on a production line somewhere). The slice of a sticky but beautifully fragrant fougasse which melts in the mouth. A sliver of pâté on a piece of rustic bread offered to tempt you into parting with a few more francs for a large jar of confit de canard by it's proud stallholder who has lovingly produced it, probably on their large kitchen table without a trace of preservatives or E numbers. And those olives! Everywhere you look, bowls and bowls of every colour and flavour. Stallholders, inviting you to help yourself until you are satisfied with your eventual choice. Where in England can you sample market produce prior to purchase. Mostly, there are signs erected everywhere warning you not to touch the produce. I wonder how a french housewife on her morning's shopping expedition would take that kind of instruction. Somehow, I don't think it would be the produce that would be pinched or squeezed.

I love the stalls quite unconnected with food whose owners, recognising the attraction of a bargain, just throw the contents of huge cardboard boxes of seconhand clothes onto the ground and erect a sign which loosely interpreted means "everything a fiver". This is when class knows no barrier! The chiquést of ladies and the stateliest of gentlemen forget their origins and POUNCE. They are all after the same thing. A bargain! An unassuming little dress that turns out to be real silk, or a crumpled sweater with the label announcing it is really cashmere or an unexpected find when someone chances upon a suit marked "designer label". It happens believe me. It is a very serious pastime in France and everyone, regardless of their background, succumbs, sooner or later.

My own weakness is for crockery. Vivid yellow and blue plates, boldly painted jugs, huge wide bowls that look like cups, oil and vinegar combinations and big brightly coloured plates. Temptation everywhere. I am generally dragged away whilst still protesting that "such and such" will look spectacular on "so and so" by my wryly amused husband. Nevertheless, my collection grows. Every piece a precious memory.

Many of the markets we have visited have been held in the most picturesque of places. Along the seafront at La Palmyre, on the quayside at Trouville, the beautiful harbour of Honfleur, through the winding streets of Frejus and completely surrounding the church at St. Jean de Monts to name but a very few. The French have a very relaxed attitude to life and there is a no more relaxing sound than the peeling of the church bells on a Sunday as the churchgoers take their leave and round off their morning of worship with a visit to their local market. En route, they will greet friends and aquintances with a round of ritual kissing. The number of kisses depends on how well they know the recipient and will begin all over again if they meet half an hour later at another place, not having neglected, of course, to kiss them all over again before they take their leave.

I wrote this book because I felt that the markets of France are special and deserve to be acknowledged for the important and unique way in which they play a part in the atmosphere that is France. Like anything " If you don't use it, you lose it". With the authorities constantly trying to enforce more and more rules and regulations on small producers, the markets of France are under threat as they have never been before. Just a short while ago I read an article on France concerning food items. It appears that all sellers will have to refrigerate their produce during sale. It does not take a huge amount of imagination to visualise what this will do to the small cheese and dairy products producers working on very small margins. What choice will they have when it comes to buying costly machinery? Whilst they are still there, I URGE YOU to patronise the small producers, wether they be markets or shops.

If you are a traveller to this exceptional country, you will already be anticipating the secrets waiting to surprise you at the next market. If you have not visited France, I envy the experience that yet awaits you. An experience that can only be described as a feast of the senses. Whoever you are, I hope you find this book as useful and as rewarding as I have found in compiling it.

Janice I. Gallagher

Hampshire

June 2001

About this book

Most markets in France start very early in the morning and unless stated, finish at noon. Where I have had this information supplied to me by the different agencies in France, I have included it in the comments box along with any other information. A note of caution here. Some communes are subject to change at short notice especially with the seasonal markets.

Where I have used the description seasonal, it can mean any time from April to September or it can be as short as July or August. I would like to have been more specific but very few departments confirmed times let alone dates. The times quoted are the twenty four hour clock.

The abbreviations used in the book are fairly easy to understand unless it is your first visit in which case they include the following;

av	avenue
bd	boulevard
mt	mont
pl	place
qrt	quartier

Some of the departments in France have not only provided me with the commune but the actual place that the market is held. Again this is subject to change but should not detour too far from the usual site. Where you see 1st and 3rd etc. it means the days in the month that the market is held and the column denotes the day.

In Paris a slightly different format has been used as the city is divided up into arrondisemonts. The comments box has been used to describe the location of the market and you will probably notice that some locations are mentioned on more than one market. This is because Paris is a very large place and means that more than one market is held at different points in the same avenue or road. Therefore, if the description mentions more than one, it is at the point where they all converge.

Some of the descriptions used for the types of market are very loosely translated to what I think is the most appropriate description, for instance, marché champêtre translated means "rustic market" or "village market" and marché campagnard is a "country market". They are sometimes also used to describe "local produce". I trust you will forgive me if my translations are inaccurate.

In the next few pages you will find some translations of items and situations you may come across in the markets. The list is not intended to be exhaustive. Nevertheless, I hope you find it useful.

The format for the lists of markets was deliberately chosen to be simple and quick to use. The book is divided up into regions first in alphabetical order followed by the departments in numerical order and then in alphabetical order of the communes. Lastly, the table consists of a weekly column and a market will appear in the column under the day or days of the week on which they are held. The last thing I wanted was for readers to have to flick back and forth with a "key to symbols page".

If there are any points you would like to make or if you would like to help in the updating of the book, I would welcome any suggestions. At the back of the book are some pages for any information you may like to make a note of and send on to me. You can write to me or e-mail me at the Publishers at loisirspublications.com

Some Useful Information

Lundi	*Monday*	Ville haute	*upper part of town*
Mardi	*Tuesday*	Ville basse	*lower part of town*
Mercredi	*Wednesday*	Banlieue	*suburbs*
Jeudi	*Thursday*		
Vendredi	*Friday*	Marché champêtre	*local produce*
Samedi	*Saturday*	Brocante	*bric-a-brac*
Dimanche	*Sunday*	Artisinal	*crafts*
Matin	*morning*	Deballage	*jumble*
Après midi	*afternoon*	Biologique	*organic*
Le soir	*evening*	Marché aux puces	*flea market*
Toute la journée	*all day long*	Marche Bouquinistes	*secondhand books*
Semaine	*weekly*	Alimentaires	*food*
Dernier	*last*	Forains	*entertainers*
Printemps	*Spring*	Marché campagnard	*country market*
Été	*Summer*	Vetêment	*clothing*
Autonne	*Autumn*		
Hiver	*Winter*		

Currency and Weight

The conversions are approxiamate and only intended for comparisons.

Ff	*French francs*
C	*centimes (100 centimes to a franc)*
113gms	*a quarter of a pound*
227gms	*a half a pound*
454gms	*a pound*
1000gms	*a kilo*
une livre	*a pound*
une demi livre	*a half a pound*
une demi kilo	*a pound*
une demi litre	*a pint*
tranche	*a slice*
morceau	*a piece*

Meat & Poultry

Agneau	*Lamb*	Mouton	*Mutton*
Andouille	*Chitterling sausage*	Oie	*Goose*
Boef	*Beef*	Perdrix	*Partridge*
Boudin blanc	*Black pudding*	Pieds de porc	*Pigs trotters*
Boudin noir	*White pudding*	Pigeon	*Pigeon*
Caille	*Quail*	Pintade	*Guinea fowl*
Canard	*Duck*	Porc	*Pork*
Cervelle	*Brains*	Poulet	*Chicken*
Charcuterie	*Cold meats*	Poussin	*Spring chicken*
Chevreuil	*Venison*	Queue de Boef	*Oxtail*
Dinde	*Turkey*	Ris de Veau	*Veal sweatbreads*
Entrecôte	*Entrecote steak*	Rognons	*Kidneys*
Faisan	*Pheasant*	Sanglier	*Wild Boar*
Foie	*Liver*	Saucisse	*Sausage*
Francfort	*Frankfurter*	Saucisson	*Cooked sausages*
Hachis	*Mince meat*	Steack	*Steak*
Jambon	*Ham*	Terrine	*Pâte*
Langue	*Tongue*	Tête de veau	*Calf's head*
Lapin	*Rabbit*	Tripes	*Tripe*
Lièvre	*Hare*	Veau	*Veal*
Merguez	*Spicy sausage*	Volaille	*Poultry*

Fish & Seafood

Aiglefin	*Haddock*	Homard	*Lobster*
Anchois	*Anchovies*	Huître	*Oysters*
Anguille	*Eel*	Langouste	*Crayfish*
Bar	*Bass*	Langoustines	*Scampi*
Barbue	*Brill*	Lieu Jaune	*Pollock*
Bouqet rose	*Prawn*	Limande	*Lemon Sole*
Brochet	*Pike*	Lotte	*Monkfish*
Bulots	*Whelks*	Loup	*Sea Bass*
Cabillaud	*Cod*	Maquereau	*Mackerel*
Calamar	*Squid*	Merlan	*Whiting*
Carpe	*Carp*	Morue	*Salt Cod*
Carrelet	*Plaice*	Moules	*Mussels*
Colin	*Hake*	Palourdes	*Clams*
Coques	*Cockles*	Perche	*Perch*
Coquilles St-Jacques	*Scallops*	Petit friture	*Whitebait*
Crabe	*Crab*	Poulpe	*Octopus*
Crevettes	*Prawns*	Raie	*Skate*
Crevettes grises	*Shrimp*	Rouget	*Red Mullet*
Cuisses de grenouille	*Frogs legs*	Rousetter	*Huss*
Daurade	*Sea Bream*	Sardine	*Sardine*
Ecrivisse	*Crayfish*	Saumon	*Salmon*
Escargots	*Snails*	Sole	*Sole*
Espadon	*Swordfish*	Thon	*Tuna*
Flétan	*Halibut*	Truite	*Trout*
Goujon	*Gudgeon*	Turbot	*Turbot*
Hareng	*Herring*		

Vegetables

Ail	Garlic	Endives	Chicory
Asperges	Asparagus	Épinards	Spinach
Artichaut	Artichoke	Fenouil	Fennel
Aubergine	Aubergine	Fèves	Broad beans
Betterave	Beetroot	Flageolets	Small kidney beans
Carottes	Carrots	Frisée	Curly endive
Céléri	Celery	Haricot	Beans
Céléri-rave	Celeriac	Laitue	Lettuce
Champignons	Mushrooms	Navet	Turnip
Chicorée	Endive	Oignon	Onion
Chou	Cabbage	Oseille	Sorrel
Choucroute	Sauerkraut	Petits pois	Peas
Chou-fleur	Cauliflower	Poireau	Leek
Chou-rave	Kohlrabi	Poivron	Sweet pepper
Choux de Bruxelles	Brussels sprouts	Pommes de terre	Potato
Coeurs de Artichaut	Artichoke hearts	Radis	Radish
Concombre	Cucumber	Tomate	Tomato
Courgette	Courgette	Topinambour	Jerusalem Artichoke
Échalotte	Shallots	Truffe	Truffle

Fruit & Nuts

Abricot	Apricot	Melon	Melon
Amandes	Almonds	Mûres	Blackberries
Ananas	Pineapple	Myrtilles	Bilberries
Arachides	Peanuts	Noisettes	Hazelnuts
Avocat	Avocado	Noix	Walnuts
Banane	Banana	Noix de Coco	Coconut
Brugnon	Nectarine	Orange	Orange
Cassis	Blackcurrant	Pamplemousse	Grapefruit
Cerises	Cherries	Pasteque	Water melon
Citron	Lemon	Pêche	Peach
Coing	Quince	Pistache	Pistachio
Dattes	Dates	Poire	Pear
Figue	Fig	Pomme	Apple
Fraise	Strawberry	Prune	Plum
Framboise	Raspberry	Pruneau	Prune
Groseilles rouges	Red currants	Raisins	Grapes
Groseilles blanches	White currants	Raisins secs	Raisins
Groseilles a maquereau	Gooseberries	Reine-claude	Greengage
Marrons	Chestnuts		

Herbs & Spices

L' Ail	*Garlic*	Menthe	*Mint*
L' Aneth	*Dill*	Muscade	*Nutmeg*
Basilic	*Basil*	Origan	*Oregano*
Cannelle	*Cinnamon*	Paprika	*Paprika*
Coriandre	*Coriander*	Piment rouge	*Chilli*
Cumin	*Cumin*	Persil	*Parsley*
Estragon	*Tarragon*	Poivre noir	*Black pepper*
Fenouil	*Fennel*	Romarin	*Rosemary*
Gingembre	*Ginger*	Sauge	*Sage*
Laurier	*Bay*	Sel	*Salt*
Marjolaine	*Marjoram*	Thym	*Thyme*
Massue	*Mace*	Vinaigre	*Vinegar*

Bread, Cakes & Confectionery

Bab au Rhum	*Rum Baba*	Massepain	*Marzipan*
Baguette	*French stick*	Milleffeuille	*Cream slice*
Barquette	*Pastry boat*	Pain	*Bread*
Beignet	*Doughnut*	Pain d'épice	*gingerbread*
Biscuit de Savoie	*Sponge cake*	Petit pain	*Bread roll*
Brioche	*Bun*	Praline	*Burnt sugar almond*
Chausson aux pommes	*Apple turnover*	Savarin	*Type of rum baba*
Chouà la crème	*Cream puff*	Tarte frangipane	*Almond cream tart*
Clafoutis	*Fruit in batter*	Tarte fraise	*Strawberry cream tart*
Croustade	*Pastry shell*	Tarte tatin	*Apple tart*
Gâteau	*Layered cake*	Tourte	*Layered cake*

International Clothing Sizes

Women's Clothes

UK	8	10	12	14	16	18	20
Bust (ins/cms)	31/80	32/82	34/87	36/92	38/97	40/102	42/109
Hips (ins/cms)	33/85	34/87	36/92	38/97	40/102	42/109	44/114

France	34	36	38	40	42	44	46
Bust (cms)	81	84	87	90	93	96	99
Hips (cms)	89	92	95	98	101	104	107

USA	8	10	12	14	16	18	20
Bust (ins)	32	33	34½	36	37½	39	41
Hips (ins)	34	35	36½	38	39½	41	43

Women's Shoe Sizes

UK	2	2½	3	3½	4	4½	5	5½	6	6½	7	7½	8
Europe	34	34½	35	35½	36½	37	37½	38	39	39½	40½	41	41½
USA	3½	4	4½	5	5½	6	6½	7	7½	8	8½	9	9½

Men's Shoe Sizes

UK	4½	5	5½	6	6½	7	7½	8	8½	9	9½	10	10½
Europe	37½	38	38½	39½	40	40½	41	42	42½	43	43½	44	44½

Men's Suits

UK/USA	36	37	38	39	40	41	42	43	44	45	46	47	48
Europe	46		48	50		52	54		56	58		60	62
(CMS)	92		96	100		104	108		112	116		120	124

The Regional Map of France

NORD -
PAS DE CALAIS

PICARDIE

NORMANDIE

CHAMPAGNE
-ARDENNES

LORRAINE

ALSACE

PARIS &
ILLE DE FRANCE

BRETAGNE

PAYS DE LOIRE

CENTRE-
VAL DE LOIRE

FRANCHE-
COMTE

BOURGOGNE

POITOU-
CHARENTE

LIMOUSIN

AUVERGNE

RHONE- ALPS

AQUITAINE

LANGUEDOC
ROUSSILLON

PROVENCE-
ALPES-COTES
D'AZURE

MIDI-PYRENEES

The Regions of France

Departments

1	Ain	Rhône - Alpes
2	Aisne	Picardie
3	Allier	Auvergne
4	Alpes de Haute Provence	Provence - Alpes - Côte d' Azur
5	Hautes Alpes	Provence - Alpes - Côte d' Azur
6	Alpes Maritimes	Provence - Alpes - Côte d' Azur
7	Ardèche	Rhône - Alpes
8	Ardennes	Champagne - Ardennes
9	Ariège Pyrénées	Midi - Pyrénées
10	Aube	Champagne - Ardennes
11	Aude	Languedoc - Roussillon
12	Aveyron	Midi - Pyrénées
13	Bouches du Rhône	Provence - Alpes - Côte d' Azur
14	Calvados	Normandie
15	Cantal	Auvergne
16	Charente	Poitou Charentes
17	Charente Maritime	Poitou Charentes
18	Cher	Centre - Val de Loire
19	Corrèze	Limousin
21	Côte d' Or	Bourgogne
22	Côtes d' Armor	Bretagne
23	Creuse	Limousin
24	Dordogne	Aquitaine
25	Doubs	Franche Comté
26	Drôme	Rhône - Alpes
27	Eure	Normandie
28	Eure et Loir	Centre - Val de Loire
29	Finistère	Bretagne
30	Gard	Languedoc - Roussillon
31	Haute Garonne	Midi - Pyrénées
32	Gers	Midi - Pyrénées
33	Gironde	Aquitaine
34	Hérault	Languedoc - Roussillon
35	Ille et Vilaine	Bretagne
36	Indre	Centre - Val de Loire
37	Indre et Loire	Centre - Val de Loire
38	Isère	Rhône - Alpes
39	Jura	Franche Comté
40	Landes	Aquitaine
41	Loir et Cher	Centre - Val de Loire
42	Loire	Rhône - Alpes
43	Haute Loire	Auvergne
44	Loire Atlantique	Pays de la Loire
45	Loiret	Centre - Val de Loire
46	Lot	Midi - Pyrénées
47	Lot et Garonne	Aquitaine
48	Lozère	Languedoc - Roussillon

Departments

49	Maine et Loire	Pays de la Loire
50	Manche	Normandie
51	Marne	Champagne - Ardennes
52	Haute Marne	Champagne - Ardennes
53	Mayenne	Pays de la Loire
54	Meurthe et Moselle	Lorraine
55	Meuse	Lorraine
56	Morbihan	Bretagne
57	Moselle	Lorraine
58	Nièvre	Bourgogne
59	Nord	Nord - Pas de Calais
60	Oise	Picardie
61	Orne	Normandie
62	Pas de Calais	Nord - Pas de Calais
63	Puy de Dôme	Auvergne
64	Pyrénées Atlantiques	Aquitaine
65	Hautes Pyrénées	Midi - Pyrénées
66	Pyrénées Orientales	Languedoc - Roussillon
67	Bas Rhin	Alsace
68	Haut Rhin	Alsace
69	Rhône	Rhône - Alpes
70	Haute Saône	Franche Comté
71	Saône et Loire	Bourgogne
72	Sarthe	Pays de la Loire
73	Savoie	Rhône - Alpes
74	Haute Savoie	Rhône - Alpes
75	Paris	Paris - Île de France
76	Seine Maritime	Normandie
77	Seine et Marne	Paris - Île de France
78	Yvelines	Paris - Île de France
79	Deux Sèvres	Poitou Charentes
80	Somme	Picardie
81	Tarn	Midi - Pyrénées
82	Tarn et Garonne	Midi - Pyrénées
83	Var	Provence - Alpes - Côte d' Azur
84	Vaucluse	Provence - Alpes - Côte d' Azur
85	Vendée	Pays de la Loire
86	Vienne	Poitou Charentes
87	Haute Vienne	Limousin
88	Vosges	Lorraine
89	Yonne	Bourgogne
90	Territoire de Belfort	Franche Comté
91	Essone	Paris - Île de France
92	Hauts de Seine	Paris - Île de France
93	Seine St-Denis	Paris - Île de France
94	Val de Marne	Paris - Île de France
95	Val d' Oise	Paris - Île de France

DEPARTMENTS

Bas Rhin	(67)
Haut Rhin	(68)

Department of Bas Rhin

Location	M	T	W	Th	F	S	Su	Comments
Andlau			•					
Barr: rue de la Kirneck					•			
Benfeld: centre ville	•							
Betschdorf					•			Local produce 1st & 3rd Saturday
Bischheim				•				
Bischwiller					•			
Bouxwiller					•			Local produce 1st & 3rd Saturday
Brumath			•					
Châtenois				•				
Dambach la Ville			•					
Dettwiller			•					
Diemeringen			•					1st Wednesday
Drulingen			•					3rd Wednesday
Duttlenheim			•					
Eckwersheim			•					
Epfig					•			Alternate Fridays
Erstein				•	•			
Fegersheim		•						
Geispolsheim					•			Small market
Gerstheim		•						1st & 3rd Tuesday
Haguenau		•			•			
Hilsenheim	•							
Hindisheim			•					
Hochfelden		•						
Hoerdt			•					Last Wednesday
Illkirch Graffenstaden			•		•			
Ingwiller					•			2nd & 4th Saturday
Kogenheim					•			1st Friday
Lauterbourg		•						
Marckolsheim			•					2nd Wednesday
Marlenheim					•			

Location	M	T	W	Th	F	S	Su	Comments
Marmoutier					•			2nd Friday 17.00 to 20.00
Mertzwiller				•				
Molsheim: pl du marché	•							
Mutzig				•				
Niederbroon				•				
Niederhaslach					•			
Ostwald				•				Afternoon
Pfaffenhoffen					•			
Plobsheim		•		•				Small markets held afternoons
Reichschoffen			•					
Rhinau		•		•				Smaller market Thursday
Rosheim				•				
Rothau					•			
Saales	•							1st Monday
Sarre Union								2nd & 4th Wednesday
Savrne		•		•		•		Health foods
Schiltigheim				•				
Schirmeck			•					
Schweighhouse sur Moder			•		•			
Sélestat		•						
Souffelweyersheim				•				
Soufflenheim			•					
Strasbourg: Allée Reuss				•				
Strasbourg: bd de la Marne		•				•		
Strasbourg: pl d'Ostwald				•				
Strasbourg: pl de Bordeaux		•				•		Health foods 9.00 to 6.00pm
Strasbourg: pl de Haldenbourg			•			•		
Strasbourg: pl de l'Ile de France				•				
Strasbourg: pl de la Gare	•			•				10.00 to 18.00 Thursday on trial
Strasbourg: pl de Wattwiller						•		
Strasbourg: pl du Corps de Garde			•			•		
Strasbourg: pl du marché Neudorf		•				•		
Strasbourg: pl du marché Neuf						•		Local produce 9.00 to 16.00
Strasbourg: pl Kléber			•		•			7.00 to 18.00
Strasbourg: Robertsau			•					14.00 to 18.00
Strasbourg: Route d'Atlenheim				•				
Strasbourg: rue de Reitwillerl			•					
Strasbourg: rue Jacob				•				
Strasbourg: rue St-Gothard Krutenau			•					
Strasbourg: rue Virgile					•			14.00 to 18.00
Strasbourg: rue Watteau			•			•		
Truchtersheim					•			Afternoon
Villé			•					
Wasselonne	•							
Westhoffen					•			1st Friday
Wissembourg						•		Local produce
Wittisheim			•	•				Health foods 2nd Thursday

Department of Haut Rhin

Location	M	T	W	Th	F	S	Su	Comments
Altkirch				•		•		Saturday regional products
Bartenheim				•				
Bergheim: pl du Docteur Walter	•							
Biesheim	•							2nd & 4th Monday
Blotzheim			•					
Bollwiller				•				
Brunstatt		•		•		•		
Burnhaupt le Bas						•		
Cernay: pl du Grun		•			•			
Chalampé			•	•	•	•		
Colmar: av de Paris			•					
Colmar: pl de l' Ancienne Douane			•					
Colmar: pl de la Cathédrale			•					Textile market open all day
Colmar: pl St-Joseph					•			
Dannemarie					•			
Ensisheim				•				
Eschentzwiller	•							2nd Monday
Ferette		•						1st Tuesday
Fessenheim		•						
Guéberschwihr	•		•					1st Monday
Guebwiller: pl de la Liberté					•			
Guebwiller: pl du Marché		•						
Hirsingue			•					
Hirtzfelden			•					
Horbourg Wihr			•					1st & 3rd Wednesday
Huningue		•		•	•	•		
Illfurth			•					
Illzach					•	•		
Ingersheim: pl de la Mairie			•					
Issenheim	•							
Kaysersberg: pl Gouraud	•							
Kingersheim		•						
Labaroche			•			•		Wednesday seasonal
Landser					•			
Lapoutroie					•			
Lièpvre	•							
Logelbach: rue Hherzog			•					Organic produce
Lutterbach			•			•		
Masevaux			•					
Merxheim		•						
Metzeral			•					
Michelbach le Bas						•		
Montreux Vieux					•			
Moosch			•					
Morschwiller le Bas					•			
Mulhouse: Canal Couvert		•		•		•		
Mulhouse: pl de l' Europe			•					Afternoon
Mulhouse: pl de la Paix					•			
Mulhouse: pl de la Réunion		•			•			

Location	M	T	W	Th	F	S	Su	Comments
Mulhouse: pl du Rattachement					•			
Munster: pl du Marché		•				•		Smaller market Tuesday
Neuf Brisach					•			
Neuf Brisach: pl d'armes	•							1st & 3rd Monday
Oberhergheim: pl de la Mairie					•			
Orbey: pl du marché			•			•		
Orschwihr				•				
Osenbach	•							
Pulversheim			•			•		
Reiningue			•					
Ribeauvillé: pl de l' Hôtel de Ville						•		
Riedisheim			•					
Riquewihr: pl des 3 Églises					•			
Rixheim				•				
Rouffach: pl de l' Église						•		
Selestat: pl d'Armes		•						
Selestat: pl de la Porte de Strasbourg		•						
Selestat: pl du Marché aux Choux		•						
Sewen Sierentz			•					
Soultz			•					
Soulxmatt		•						
St-Amarin	•							
St-Hyppolite					•			
St-Louis				•		•		
Staffelfelden		•				•		
Ste-Croix aux Mines						•		
Ste-Croix en Plaine		•						
Ste-Marie aux Mines						•		
Steinbach					•			Afternoon
Thann: parking stade Lang			•					Small market
Thann: pl du Bungert						•		
Turckheim: pl de la République					•			
Wattwiller				•	•			Friday alternate weeks
Wettolsheim: pl du Général de Gaulle			•					
Widensolen: pl du Village						•		
Wihr au Val				•				
Willer sur Thur				•				
Wintzenheim: Logelbach			•					
Wintzenheim: pl des Fêtes					•			
Wittelsheim				•				
Wittenheim						•		
Wuenheim					•			

DEPARTMENTS

Dordogne	(24)
Gironde	(33)
Landes	(40)
Lot et Garonne	(47)
Pyrénées-Atlantiques	(64)

Department of Dordogne								
Location	M	T	W	Th	F	S	Su	Comments
Abjat		•						Last Tuesday
Beaumont					•			
Belvès					•			
Bergerac			•		•			
Bergerac: Naillac							•	
Bergerac: PL Barbacane				•				
Bergerac: pl des 2 Conils					•			
Bergerac: pl du Marché			•		•			
Bergerac: pL Gambetta			•		•			
Bergerac: rue de la Résistance			•		•			
Brantôme					•			Walnut fair Friday October & November
Bussière Badil			•					2nd & 4th Wednesday
Cadouin			•					
Champagnac de Belair	•							1st Monday
Coulounieix Chamiers		•			•	•		
Couze et St-Front							•	
Creysse							•	
Domme				•				
Excideuil				•				
Eymet				•			•	Sunday seasonal
Gardonne			•				•	
Génis	•							2nd Monday
Hautefort	•		•					1st Monday
Issigeac							•	
Javrlhac				•				2nd Thursday
Jumilhac le Grand			•					2nd & 4th Wednesday
La Coquille				•				
La Force				•				
La Roche Chalais				•		•		1st Thursday
La Rochebeaucourt				•				1st Thursday
Lalinde				•				

Location	M	T	W	Th	F	S	Su	Comments
Lanouaille		•						2nd & 4th Tuesday
Le Bugue: pl de la Mairie		•				•		
Le Buisson de Cadouin					•			
Le Fleix	•							
Le Lardin St-Lazare					•			
Les Eyzies de Tayac	•							
Lisle		•						Poultry & walnuts in October & November
Mareuil		•						28th
Miallet	•							3rd Monday
Monpazier				•		•		
Montignac			•			•		Walnuts on Wednesday in Oct & Nov
Montpon Ménestérol			•					
Mouleydier			•					
Mussidan						•		
Neuvic		•				•		
Nontron						•		18th
Payzac		•						1st & 3rd Tuesday
Périgueux			•			•		Truffles from November to February
Piégut Pluviers			•					
Port Ste-Foy Ponchapt		•						
Pressignac Vicq							•	seasonal
Prigonrieux		•					•	
Ribérac			•		•			Walnuts from November to February
Rouffignac							•	
Salignac Eyvigues					•			Last Friday
Sarlat la Canéda			•			•		
Sigoules					•			
Singleyrac							•	seasonal
Siorac en Périgord			•					
Sorges					•			
St-Astier				•				
St-Aulaye		•				•		Last Tuesday
St-Cyprien			•				•	2nd Monday
St-Léon sur l'Isle					•			Evening
St-Pardoux la Rivière		•				•	•	2nd Tuesday
St-Pompont								29th
St-Saud Lacoussière	•							Last Monday
Ste-Alvère	•							Organic food July to August Truffles between December & March
Terrasson la Villedieu				•				
Thenon; pl de la Mairie		•						Truffles & poultry fair November to February
Thiviers						•		
Tocane St-Apre: pl des Tilleuls	•							Walnut fair October & November
Trémolat		•						
Varaignes	•							5th
Vélines			•					
Vergt					•			
Verteillac						•		Evening
Villamblard	•							
Villefranche de Lonchat: pl de la Liberté		•						

Department of Gironde

Location	M	T	W	Th	F	S	Su	Comments
Andernos: pl du 14 Juillet		•		•	•	•		covered market
Arcachon: la Mairie	•	•	•	•	•	•	•	covered market open 7.00 - 13.00
Arcs		•						
Aubiers: av Laroque					•			Country market
Audenge: place de l'Église		•						
Bacalan: bd Brandebourg				•				
Bazas						•		Country market
Blaye			•			•		Traditional market on Sunday
Bordeaux: de la Bastide pl Carmelle				•				
Bordeaux: des Chartrons		•	•		•	•	•	
Bordeaux: des Grands Hommes	•	•	•	•	•	•		covered market open all day
Bordeaux: du Grand Parc					•			
Bordeaux: marché de Lerme			•					
Bordeaux: marché Victor Hugo	•	•	•	•	•			covered market open 6.00 - 14.00
Bordeaux: pl Meynard	•				•			
Bordeaux: pl Meynard-Canteloup					•			
Bordeaux: pl St-Pierre			•					Organic food
Bordeaux: St-Jean Belcier		•						
Bordeaux: St-Martial			•					Country market
Bordeaux: St-Michel		•			•			Organic food
Bordeaux: St-Seurin				•				organic food
Bordeaux: St-Victor Dupeux pl d'Arlac		•						
Bourg sur Gironde							•	
Cap Ferrat	•	•	•	•	•	•	•	Summer markets Wednesday in winter
Captieux: pl de la Mairie	•							covered market open 7.00 - 13.00
Castillon la Bataille: centre ville	•						•	Flowers on Sunday
Cauderan: pl des Pins Francs			•					
Cauderan: pl St-Armand					•			Organic food
Claouey	•	•	•	•	•	•	•	Summer markets
Coutras			•		•			
Créon: pl de la Prévôté			•					
Eysines: pl du General de Gaulle				•				
Eysines: pl Floral Migron							•	
Gujan Mestras: Mairie			•					
Hourtin: pl de l' Église		•	•			•	•	Wednesday afternoon in season
La Teste de Buch: centre ville	•	•	•	•	•	•	•	covered market
Lacanau: Océan: pl de l'Europe			•					
Lacanau: Ville: pl de la Gaiété		•						
Lesparre: pl du Mal Foch		•			•	•		1st Friday market & fair
Lesparre: pl Gambetta					•			
Libourne: pl centrale		•			•		•	
Merignac Mondésir							•	
Merignac: pl de l' Église			•		•			
Monségur	•	•			•			Monday food market 1st June to 1st September
Pauillac: pl de l' Église					•			
Pessac: centre George Pompidou			•		•		•	Wednesday organic food
Piraillan	•	•	•	•	•	•	•	Summer markets
Podensac: pl Gambetta		•			•			

Location	M	T	W	Th	F	S	Su	Comments
Sauveterre de Guyenne: pl de la République		•						
Soulac sur Mer	•	•	•	•	•	•	•	covered market
St-André de Cubzac: champ de Foire				•		•		
St-Savin: pl du Faure	•							
Ste-Foy la Grande: Mairie	•	•	•	•	•	•	•	covered market open 8.00 - 13.00
Talence Thouars							•	
Talence: pl de l' Église					•			
Targon: pl de l' Eglise	•			•				
Vendays Montalivet	•	•	•	•	•	•	•	15th June to 15th September
Villandraut: pl du bourg				•				

Department of Landes

Location	M	T	W	Th	F	S	Su	Comments
Aire sur l'Adour: pl du G. de Gaulle		•				•		
Amou: pl de la Tecouere							•	
Azur		•						
Biscarrosse					•		•	Daily in season
Capbreton: allées Morines		•		•		•		Daily in season
Castets				•				
Dax					•			
Eugénie les Bains			•					seasonal
Gabarret			•					Evening
Geaune				•				Every 15 days
Grenade sur l'Adour: pl des Tilleuls	•							
Habas					•			
Hagetmau			•					
Labastide d'Armagnac	•							July & August
Labenne		•			•			
Labouheyre				•				
Léon: pl de la Poste		•						Daily in season
Linxe		•			•			
Lit et Mixe: petite place		•						1st & 3rd Tuesday. Daily in season
Luxey				•				2nd Thursday
Magescq				•				
Messanges			•			•		seasonal
Mimizan				•	•			Thursday seasonal
Moliets et Maa: plage		•		•		•		seasonal
Mont de Marsan: pl des Arenes		•	•			•		1st Wednesday
Montfort en Chalosse			•					
Morcenx			•			•		
Mugron				•				
Oeyreluy		•		•				
Parentis en Born		•		•	•			Tuesday evening & Saturday in season
Peyrehorade			•			•		
Pomarez: pl des Arènes	•			•				
Pontenx les Forges					•			
Pontonx		•						
Rion des Landes				•				
Roquefort					•			
Sabres				•				

Location	M	T	W	Th	F	S	Su	Comments
Sanguinet			•		•			Wednesday seasonal
Seignosse: allées centrale		•						
Soorts Hossegor	•		•		•		•	Monday Wednesday & Friday seasonal
Sore				•				
Soustons: pl des Arenes	•			•				Thursday seasonal
St-Julien en Born	•	•	•	•	•	•	•	July & August
St-Martin de Seignanx					•			
St-Paul les Dax				•				
St-Sever					•			
St-Vincent de Tyrosse				•				
Tarnos					•			
Tartas: allées Marines	•				•			Saturday seasonal
Vielle St-Gisons							•	
Vieux Boucau		•			•			daily in season
Villeneuve de Marsan			•					
Ychoux					•			
Ygos							•	

Department of Lot et Garonne

Location	M	T	W	Th	F	S	Su	Comments
Agen: Esplanade du Gravier						•		Local produce
Agen: Halle du Pin		•					•	Local produce
Agen: pl des Laitiers						•		Local produce & organic food
Aiguillon: pl du 14 Juillet		•			•			
Astaffort: Halle de la Mairie						•		
Astaffort: pl A.Routié	•							
Beauville							•	Local produce 15th June to 15th September
Beauville: pl de la Mairie							•	Local produce
Cancon: pl de la Halle	•							
Cancon: pl du Foirail	•							2nd, 4th & 5th Monday Veal, 1st & 3rd Monday sheep
Castillonnès		•			•			Friday July to August
Clairac				•				seasonal
Duras: les Halles	•			•		•		Traditional market Thursday & Saturday from June to September
Frespech					•			Local produce July to August
Fumel							•	
Lacapelle Biron: pl du marché	•							Local produce
Lavardac: village			•					Local produce June to September
Mézin: pl Armand Fallières				•			•	Local produce Sundays large market with entertainments
Miramont: pl de la Mairie	•				•			
Monflanquin: pl des Arcades		•		•		•		seasonal
Monsempron Libos				•				
Nerac: en ville					•			
Nerac: Quai de la Baïse		•						Evening 17.00 to 22.00 June to September
Penne d`Agenais							•	
Pujols							•	
Tournon d`Agenais: village					•			Thursday seasonal
Villeneuve sur Lot: pl d'Aquitaine			•					Organic food

Location	M	T	W	Th	F	S	Su	Comments
Villeneuve sur Lot: pl Lafayette		•			•			Traditional market
Villeneuve sur Lot: Tour de Paris					•			Local produce evening 17.00 to 19.00

Department of Pyrénées Atlantiques

Location	M	T	W	Th	F	S	Su	Comments
Aramits							•	
Arthez de Béarne: pl de la Mairie					•			
Artix: pl de la Mairie			•					
Arudy: pl de la Mairie		•			•			
Arzacq Arraziguet: pl de la République					•			
Bayonne	•	•	•	•	•	•	•	
Bedous			•					Also evenings July to August
Biarritz	•	•	•	•	•	•	•	
Billère					•			
Eaux Bonnes			•					July & August
Etsaut							•	July & August
Gan			•					
Garlin			•					Alternate Wednesdays
Hendaye			•		•			
Laruns					•			
Lasseube					•			
Lembeye				•				
Lestelle Betharam								Evening July & August
Mauléon		•			•			
Monein: pl de la Mairie	•							
Montardon					•			
Morlaàs					•	•		
Mourenx			•		•			
Navarrenx			•					
Nay		•						
Oloron Ste-Marie				•				
Orthez		•			•			
Pau: pl M. Laborde	•	•	•	•	•	•	•	Chestnuts, Foie gras etc.
Pontacq					•			
Salies de Béarn				•	•			
Sauvagnon							•	
Sauveterre			•		•			
Soumoulou					•			Alternate Fridays
St-Jean de Luz	•	•	•	•	•	•	•	Daily in season
St-Jean Pied de Port: centre ville	•							
St-Palais					•			
Tardets Sorholus: pl centrale	•							Alternate Mondays
Urrugne			•		•			Livestock on 2nd Friday

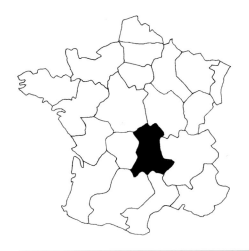

DEPARTMENTS

Allier	(3)
Cantal	(15)
Haute Loire	(43)
Puy de Dôme	(63)

Department of Allier

Location	M	T	W	Th	F	S	Su	Comments
Abrest							•	Morning
Ainay le Château		•						Morning
Arfeuilles			•					
Beaulon	•	•						4th Tuesday morning
Bellenavs			•					Morning
Bellerive sur Allier: pl de la Source Intermittente		•			•			
Bessay			•					Morning
Bézenet		•						
Bourbon l'Archambault					•			
Broût Vernet				•				
Buxières les Mines			•					
Cérilly				•				
Chantelle				•				Morning
Chazemais				•				
Chevagnes	•							3rd Monday
Commentry					•			Morning
Cosne d'Allier: rue du marché		•						
Cusset					•			
Désertines				•				Evening
Diou	•							1st Monday
Domérat					•			
Dompierre sur Besbre					•			
Doyet				•				Morning
Ébreuil				•				
Gannat		•			•			Morning
Gannay sur Loire	•							4th Monday
Hérisson					•			Morning
Huriel		•						
Jaligny sur Besbre		•						Morning
La Chapelaude							•	Morning
Lapalisse				•				

Location	M	T	W	Th	F	S	Su	Comments
Le Donjon		•						
Le Mayet de Montagne	•							
Le Montet				•				Evening
Lurcy Lévis: pl de la Mairie	•							
Marcillat en Combraille				•				
Meaulne	•							
Montaiguët en Forez			•					
Montluçon: Bien Assis					•			
Montluçon: Fontbouillant		•						
Montluçon: Montmarault			•					
Montluçon: pl de la Fraternitè				•				
Montluçon: pl Marx Dormoy						•		
Montluçon: pl Piquant						•		
Montluçon: Villegozet			•				•	
Moulins: pl d'Allier		•			•			Tuesday morning
Moulins: pl de la Liberté				•				
Moulins: pl de Lattre de Tassigny				•				
Néris les Bains				•			•	Morning
Neuilly le Réal				•				
Noyant d'Allier			•					
Souvigny				•				
St-Bonnet Troncais				•				
St-Désiré			•					
St-Germain des Fossés				•				
St-Menoux			•					
St-Pourçain sur Sioule						•		
St-Sauvier	•							
St-Yorre			•					
Thiel sur Acolin			•					1st Wednesday
Treignat				•				
Tronget	•							
Urçay				•				
Vallon en Sully		•						
Varennes sur Allier: centre ville		•						
Vichy		•	•	•		•		
Villefranche d'Allier	•							
Viplaix			•					
Ygrande			•					Morning
Yzeure			•					

Department of Cantal

Location	M	T	W	Th	F	S	Su	Comments
Allanche		•						seasonal
Aurillac			•			•		
Chalvignac						•		seasonal 18.00 & 22.00
Champs sur Tarentaine						•		July & August 18.00 to 22.00
Chapelle Laurent					•			1st Friday
Chaudes Aigues	•							
Cheylade						•		July & August 18.00 to 23.00
Condat						•		

Location	M	T	W	Th	F	S	Su	Comments
Favrolles	•							1st Monday
Fontagnes							•	from 18.30 to 22.00
Lacapelle Barrès	•							1st Monday
Lafeuillade en Vézie							•	July & August 18.00 to 22.00
Lorcières					•			1st Friday
Mandailles St-Julien							•	July & August 18.00 to 21.30
Massiac: pl Manclin	•	•						
Mauriac		•		•	•			
Maurines					•			1st Friday
Maurs				•				
Murat			•					July to September until 18.00
Neussargues Moissac				•				from 17.00 to 19.30
Neuveglise				•				
Pierrefort			•					seasonal
Pleaux					•	•		Friday 19.00 to 23.00 in July & August
Polminhac					•			seasonal
Quezac							•	July & August until 18.00
Riom ès Montagnes								15th
Salers			•					
St-Amandin				•				July to September until 18.00
St-Cernin							•	seasonal
St-Flour		•						July & August 17.00 to 20.00
St-Mamet					•			July & August 18.30 to 22.00
St-Martin la Salvetat							•	July & August until 19.00
St-Paul de Salers				•				from 18.00 to 22.00
St-Vincent: la Vallee du Mars					•			July & August 18.30 to 22.00
Talizat	•							1st Monday
Trizac							•	seasonal
Vic sur Cère: pl du Carladez		•			•			
Vigean					•			from 18.30 to 24.00
Ydes							•	seasonal

Department of Haute Loire

Location	M	T	W	Th	F	S	Su	Comments
Allègre			•					
Aurec sur Loire			•		•		•	
Auzon	•	•	•	•	•	•	•	
Bas en Basset			•					
Beauzac							•	
Blesle: marché de pays					•			July & August
Brioude						•		
Chaise Dieu				•				
Champagnac le Vieux				•				
Chomelix				•				July & August
Costaros	•							Large lively market, entertainers & livestock
Craponne sur Arzon						•		
Dunières				•				
Fay sur Lignon			•				•	
Landos		•						
Langeac		•		•				

Location	M	T	W	Th	F	S	Su	Comments
Lapte						•		
Laussonne			•					
Lavoûte Chilhac							•	
Le Chambon sur Lignon					•			
Le Monastier sur Gazeille		•					•	
Le Puy en Velay: pl du Plot l'Italienne					•			
Lempdes		•						
Les Estables				•			•	
Loude		•						1st & 3rd Tuesday
Mazet St-Voy				•				
Montfaucon en Velay			•					
Paulhaguet	•							
Retournac				•				Entertainers in July & August
Riotord					•			
Saugues	•				•			
Siaugues Ste-Marie							•	
Solignac sur Loire			•					
St-Bonnet le Froid				•				
St-Jean Lachalm					•			
St-Julien Chapteuil	•							
St-Pal de Mons				•			•	
St-Pierre du Champ							•	
Ste-Sigolène		•						
Tence: centre ville		•						
Vorey sur Arazon							•	
Yssingeaux				•		•		

Department of Puy de Dôme

Location	M	T	W	Th	F	S	Su	Comments
Aigueperse		•						
Ambert: centre ville				•				
Ardes sur Couze	•							
Arlanc: centre ville	•							
Aubière: pl de la Libération					•		•	Sunday morning
Aulnat: place de l'Eglise			•					
Aydat		•						seasonal
Beaumont					•			
Beauregard l' Évêque					•	•		
Besse en Chandesse	•							Cheese market
Billom: centre ville	•							
Blot l' Église		•						4th Tuesday
Brassac les Mines							•	
Cébazat			•				•	
Ceyrat					•			
Chamalières		•		•	•		•	Friday evening
Chambon sur Lac					•			seasonal
Champeix					•			
Chapdes Beaufort							•	1st Sunday
Charbonnier les Mines					•			
Châteaugay							•	

Location	M	T	W	Th	F	S	Su	Comments
Châteldon							•	
Chauriat					•			
Clermont Ferrand: av du Puy-de-Dôme		•						Food only
Clermont Ferrand: Espace St-Pierre	•	•	•	•	•	•		All day except Sunday
Clermont Ferrand: Flamina			•					
Clermont Ferrand: Halles St-Joseph		•			•			Tuesday afternoon
Clermont Ferrand: Herbet			•					
Clermont Ferrand: La Glacière		•			•			
Clermont Ferrand: La Plaine		•						
Clermont Ferrand: Les Landais		•		•	•			
Clermont Ferrand: Loucheur			•					
Clermont Ferrand: Neuf Soleils		•		•	•			
Clermont Ferrand: pl de Regensburg			•					
Clermont Ferrand: pl de Verdun			•		•			Friday 15.00 to 20.00
Clermont Ferrand: pl du Mazet					•			
Clermont Ferrand: pl Littré			•		•			
Clermont Ferrand: pl Poly				•				
Coudes			•					
Cournon d'Auvergne			•	•	•			
Courpière		•						
Cunlhat			•					
Égliseneuve d'Entraigues			•					Cheese market
Égliseneuve près Billom							•	seasonal
Ennezat			•					
Gerzat				•			•	
Giat								Many markets & fairs frequently through the year
Issoire					•			
Job							•	
Jumeaux		•						
La Bourboule					•			
La Monnerie le Montel					•			
La Roche Blanche		•						
La Tour d'Auvergne		•			•			
Le Breuil sur Couze			•					
Le Cendre				•				
Le Mont Dore				•				
Lempdes		•			•			
Les Ancizes Comps			•					
Les Martres de Veyre			•					
Lezoux						•		
Manzat			•					
Maringues: centre ville	•							
Marsac en Livradois							•	
Menat			•				•	
Mezel				•				
Montaigut en C'brailles		•						
Montferrand: La Rodade				•				
Murol			•					
Nohanent		•						
Olliergues					•			

Location	M	T	W	Th	F	S	Su	Comments
Orcet		•						
Pérignat Sarliève		•			•			
Peschadoires							•	
Pionsat					•			1st Friday
Pont du Château				•				
Pontaumur			•					
Pontgibaud				•				
Puy Guillaume			•					
Randan					•			3rd Friday
Riom						•		
Romagnat								7th & 13th of the month
Royat: pl Jean Cohendy		•			•			
Sauxillanges		•						2nd & 4th Tuesday
St-Amant Tallende		•			•			
St-Anthème		•						2nd & 4th Tuesday
St-Dier d'Auvergne				•				
St-Éloy les Mines					•			
St-Georges de Mons				•				
St-Germain Lembron		•						
St-Gervais d'Auvergne: pl de la Liberté	•							
St-Nectaire							•	seasonal
St-Rémy sur Durolle				•			•	
Tauves				•				1st Thursday
Thiers	•		•	•	•			
Vernet la Varenne	•							1st & 3rd Monday
Vertaizon				•				
Vertolaye						•		
Vic le Comte				•		•		
Viverols		•						1st & 3rd Tuesday
Volvic					•		•	

DEPARTMENTS

Côte d'Or	(21)
Nièvre	(58)
Saône et Loire	(71)
Yonne	(89)

Department of Côte d'Or

Location	M	T	W	Th	F	S	Su	Comments
Aignay le Duc					•			
Arnay le Duc			•					
Auxonne: pl d'Armes					•			
Beaune			•		•			
Bligny sur Ouche			•					
Brazey en Plaine			•					Last Wednesday
Châtillon sur Seine					•			
Chenôve			•				•	
Dijon: Halles Centralles				•	•			
Epoisses			•					Wednesday afternoon
Genlis					•			
Gevrey Chambertin		•						
Grancey le Château							•	
Is sur Tille			•		•			1st Wednesday
La Roche en Brenil			•					
Laignes					•			
Lamarche sur Saône		•			•			Saturday afternoon & 3rd Tuesday
Longvic				•			•	
Marsannay la Côte				•	•			
Meursalt				•				
Mirebeau sur Bèze			•					
Montbard					•			
Nolay	•							
Nuits St-Georges					•			
Pontailler sur Saône					•			
Pouilly en Auxois			•					2nd Thursday
Précy sous Thil		•						3rd Tuesday
Quetigny			•				•	Wednesday afternoon
Recey sur Ource					•			
Rouvray							•	2nd Sunday
Ruffey les Echirey							•	

Location	M	T	W	Th	F	S	Su	Comments
Saulieu				•		•		
Selongey						•		
Semur en Auxois				•	•		•	Sunday from 3rd May to 27th September
Sennecey les Dijon						•		
Seurre					•	•		3rd Friday
Sombernon				•				Afternoon
St-Apollinaire			•					
St-Jean de Losne						•		
Talant					•			Afternoon
Venarey les Laumes			•					
Vitteaux						•		

Department of Nièvre

Location	M	T	W	Th	F	S	Su	Comments
Château Chinon						•		
Châtillon en Bazois		•						
Clamecy						•		
Corbigny	•	•			•			2nd Tuesday Cattle market Monday after-
noons								
Cosne sur Loire			•		•		•	
Decize		•			•			3rd Tuesday
Donzy				•	•			
Dornes			•					
Guérigny			•		•			
Imphy			•		•			
La Charité sur Loire						•		
La Machine						•		
Lormes				•				
Luzy				•				
Moulins Engilbert	•	•		•		•		Cattle Monday & Tuesday
Nevers: marché Banlay				•				
Nevers: marché Carnot		•	•	•	•	•		
Nevers: marché Montôt				•				
Nevers: marché St-Arigle		•	•	•	•	•		
Pougues les Eaux				•				
Pouilly sur Loire					•			
Prémery		•				•		
St-Amand en Puisaye: pl du marché	•							
St-Benin d'Azy	•							
St-Honoré les Bains				•				seasonal
St-Pierre le Moûtier				•				
Tannay							•	
Varzy				•				

Department of Saône et Loire

Location	M	T	W	Th	F	S	Su	Comments
Autun: pl du Champ de Mars			•		•			
Beaurepaire en Bresse			•					
Bellevesvre					•			

Location	M	T	W	Th	F	S	Su	Comments
Blanzy		•						
Bourbon Lancy					•			
Buxy			•					
Chagny							•	
Chalon sur Saône					•		•	
Chapelle de Guinchay							•	
Charnay lès Mâcon					•		•	Friday 14.30 to 19.00
Charolles		•						
Chauffailles					•			
Ciry le Noble					•			
Cluny					•			
Couches		•						
Cuiseaux					•			
Cuisery		•						
Digoin							•	
Ecuisses							•	
Épinac					•			
Gergy		•						
Gibles							•	
Givry			•					
Gueugnon			•					
La Chapelle de Guinchay							•	
La Clayette		•						
La Roche Vineuse			•					
Le Creusot		•	•		•			
Louhans: pl Thibert	•							
Lugny					•			
Mâcon					•			
Marcigny	•							
Martailly lès Brancion							•	
Matour			•					
Melay					•			
Mervans					•			
Montceau les Mines		•	•		•			
Montchanin			•					
Montpont en Bresse			•					
Palinges					•			
Paray le Monial					•			
Perrecy les Forges					•			
Pierre de Bresse: rue de Thiard	•							
Pont de Veyle	•							
Romanèche Thorins			•					
Romenay					•			
Sagy			•					
Salornay sur Guye			•					
Sanvignes les Mines				•				
Sennecey le Grand				•				
Senozan				•				
Simandre			•					
St-Bonnet de Joux					•			
St-Christophe en Brionnais			•					

Location	M	T	W	Th	F	S	Su	Comments
St-Gengoux le National		•						
St-Germain du Bois					•			
St-Germain du Plain				•				
St-Léger sur Dheune		•						
St-Marcel			•					
St-Martin en Bresse			•					
St-Usage					•			
St-Vallier		•			•			
Thoissey				•				
Torcy			•					
Toulon sur Arroux	•							
Tournus						•		
Uchizy							•	
Varennes St-Sauveur				•				
Verdun sur le Doubs				•				
Viré				•				

Department of Yonne

Location	M	T	W	Th	F	S	Su	Comments
Aillant sur Tholon; Thierry Ruby		•						
Ancy le Franc: pl Clermont Tonnerre				•				
Auxerre: centre ville			•					
Auxerre: pl Arquebuse		•			•			
Auxerre: Zup							•	
Avallon: l'Hopital					•			
Cerisiers							•	
Chablis							•	
Charny		•					•	
Chéroy		•						
Dixmont							•	
Domats							•	
Joigny		•			•			
Migennes				•				
Monéteau					•			
Pont sur Yonne		•					•	
Quarré les Tombes		•						
Seignelay				•			•	
Sens: centre ville	•				•			
Sens: zup			•					
St-Clement				•				
St-Fargeau					•			
St-Florentin: pl Dubost & Dilo	•					•		
St-Julien du Sault				•			•	
Tonnerre						•		
Toucy						•		
Veron		•				•		Tuesdays seasonal
Villeneuve l'Archevêque						•		
Villeneuve sur Yonne	•				•			

DEPARTMENTS

Côtes d'Armor	(22)
Finistère	(29)
Ille et Vilaine	(35)
Morbihan	(56)

Department of Côtes d'Armor

Location	M	T	W	Th	F	S	Su	Comments
Bégard					•			
Belle Isle en Terre			•					
Binic				•	•			Friday evening in season
Bourbriac		•						
Broons			•					
Callac			•					
Caulnes		•						
Châtelaudren: pl de la République	•							
Dinan				•	•			Friday evening at Marché au
Manoir.Handicrafts & food specialities								
Erquy					•			
Étables sur Mer: pl Jean Heurtel		•			•			Saturday seasonal
Fréhel		•						
Guingamp				•	•			
Ile de Bréhat	•	•	•	•	•	•	•	July & August
Jugon les Lacs					•			
La Roche Derrien					•			
Lamballe			•					
Lancieux: pl de l'Eglise		•						Summer
Lannion: pl du Centre				•				All day flower market
Lanvollon					•			
Lézardrieux					•			
Loguivy Plougras					•			
Louargat			•					
Loudéac				•		•		Local produce Thursday evening
Matignon			•					
Merdrignac			•					
Mûr de Bretagne					•			18.00 to 22.00 in summer
Paimpol: pl du marché Gambetta		•						
Penvénan					•			
Perret: Pâques â la Toussaint							•	

Location	M	T	W	Th	F	S	Su	Comments
Perros Guirec: La Clarte					•		•	Sunday April to October
Plancoët					•			
Planguenoual	•							17.00 to 20.30 July to August
Plédran					•			
Pléneuf Val Andre de Nantais		•			•			Friday April to September
Plérin						•		
Plestin les Grèves		•					•	Tuesday evening July to August
Pleubian					•			
Plouaret: pl de l'Eglise		•						
Ploubalay					•			
Ploubazlanec	•	•	•	•	•	•	•	Every evening 17..00 to 19.00 in summer
Plouec sur Lié			•					
Plouër sur Rance						•		July & August
Plouézec					•			
Ploufragan Plurien					•			July & August
Plouha			•					
Ploumilliau					•			
Pontrieux: pl de la Mairie	•							
Pordic					•			
Quintin		•						
Rostrenen		•						
St-Brieuc			•		•			
St-Brieuc : Croix St-Lambert						•		
St-Cast le Guildo	•				•			Mondays 15/6 - 15/9. Local produce Friday evenings
St-Jacut de la Mer					•			
St-Juvat					•			Friday 16.00 to 20.00 from June to September
St-Michel en Grève	•							
St-Quay Portrieux: le Port	•							
Taden					•			17.00 to 22.00 June to August
Trébeurden		•						
Trégastel: pl Ste-Anne	•							
Trégueux					•			
Tréguier			•					

Department of Finistère

Location	M	T	W	Th	F	S	Su	Comments
Audierne: centre					•			
Bannalec			•					2nd & 4th Wednesday
Bénodet: pl du Meneyer	•							
Brasparts	•							1st Monday
Brest: pl de la Liberté & av Clemenceau	•	•						Tuesday evening
Briec				•				1st Tuesday
Brignonan Plages				•				July & August
Camaret sur Mer		•						3rd Tuesday Daily in season
Carantec			•					
Carhaix				•				
Châteaulin			•				•	Sunday Seasonal
Châteauneuf du Faou			•					1st, 3rd & 5th Wednesday

Location	M	T	W	Th	F	S	Su	Comments
Cléden Cap Sizun				•				4th Thursday
Cléder					•		•	Sunday Seasonal
Clohars Carnoët					•			
Combrit			•					
Concarneau	•				•			
Crozon			•					2nd & 4th Wednesday
Daoulas							•	
Dinéault		•			•			
Douarnenez: centre ville	•							
Ergué Gabéric		•						3rd Tuesday
Fouesnant les Glénan					•			
Guerlesquin: pl du Martroy	•							
Guilers					•			
Guipavas					•			
Huelgoat				•				
Ile d'Ouessant			•			•		Evening Mussels
Ile Tudy	•							July & August
Kerhuon					•			
L' Hôpital Camfrout				•				
La Forêt-Fouesnant		•					•	Tuesday evening
Lampaul Plouarzel				•				
Landéda		•						
Landerneau	•	•			•	•		
Landivisiau			•					
Lanmeur					•			
Lannilis			•					
Le Conquet: rue Poncelin		•						
Le Faou		•				•		Last Saturday
Le Guilvinec		•				•	•	Sunday seasonal
Le Relecq					•			
Lesneven	•							All day
Locmaria Plouzané			•					
Locquirec			•					
Loctudy: pl des Anciens Combattants		•						
Melgven					•			
Moëlan sur Mer: pl de l'Eglise		•						
Morlaix			•		•			
Névez					•			
Penm'che Kérity					•			15th June to 15th September
Pleyben		•			•			2nd Tuesday
Plobannalec Lesconil			•					
Plogoff				•				
Plogonnec				•				
Plomodiern					•			1st Friday
Plonéour Lanvern					•			Last Friday
Plonévez du Faou					•			2nd Friday
Plonevez Porzay		•						3rd Tuesday July & August Local Produce
Ploudalmézeau				•				
Plouescat						•		
Plougasnou		•						
Plougastel Daoulas				•				

Location	M	T	W	Th	F	S	Su	Comments
Plougonvelin							•	
Plougonven		•						
Plouguerneau				•				
Plouguerneau Lilia		•						Tuesday evening July to August
Plouhinec							•	July & August
Plouigneau							•	
Plounéour Trez					•			July & August
Plouzané			•					
Plozévet	•							1st Monday
Pont Aven		•						
Pont Croix					•			1st & 3rd Thursday
Pont l'Abbé					•			
Primelin					•			July & August
Quimper		•			•	•	•	Friday evening
Quimperlé					•			
Riec sur Belon			•		•			
Roscoff			•					
Rosporden					•			
Santec						•	•	Sunday Seasonal
Scaër					•			
Sizun					•			1st Friday
Spézet					•			Last Friday
St-Guénolé					•			
St-Martin des Champs							•	
St-Nicolas Pentrez	•	•	•	•	•	•	•	July & August
St-Pol de Léon		•						
St-Renan						•		
Telgruc sur Mer		•			•			
Treffiagat						•		
Trégourez					•			3rd Friday
Trégunc		•	•				•	Tuesday evening & Sunday in July & August

Department of Ille et Vilaine

Location	M	T	W	Th	F	S	Su	Comments
Acigné			•					
Antrain		•						
Argentré du Plessis: pl de la Poste				•				
Bain de Bretagne: pl de la République	•							
Bazouges la Pérouse				•				
Beaucé				•				
Bécherel						•	•	1st Sunday for Books
Bédée						•		
Betton							•	
Bréal sous Montfort				•				
Bruz				•				
Cancale							•	
Cesson Sévigné				•				
Chartres de Bretagne				•				
Châteaubourg			•					
Châteaugiron				•				

Location	M	T	W	Th	F	S	Su	Comments
Chavagne			•					
Combourg: pl A.Parent & rue Notre Dame	•							
Corps Nuds			•					
Dinard: parc des Tourelles		•	•	•		•	•	Wednesday seasonal
Dol de Bretagne						•		
Fougères				•	•	•		Livestock
Gaël					•			
Goven			•					
Guichen: pl Georges le Cornec		•						
Guignen			•					
Guipry				•				
Hédé		•						
Iffendic						•		
Irodouer				•				
Janzé			•					
L' Hermitage						•		
La Bouexière						•		
La Chapelle des Fougeretz						•		
La Guerche de Bretagne: centre ville		•						
La Méziere							•	
La Richardais							•	
Langouet				•				
Le Grand Frougeray						•		
Le Pertre			•					
Le Rheu								
Lécousse							•	
Liffré					•			
Lohéac						•		
Louvigné du Désert					•			
Martigné Ferchaud					•			
Maure de Bretagne							•	
Melesse			•					
Miniac Morvan					•			
Montauban de Bretagne			•					
Montfort sur Meu					•			
Mordelles: pl de l'Eglise		•						
Noyal Châtillon sur Seiche							•	
Noyal sur Vilaine: pl de l'Eglise		•						
Pacé			•					
Pipriac: pl de Verdun		•						
Pleine Fougères		•						
Plélan le Grand							•	
Plerguer			•					
Pleurtuit					•			
Redon: pl Duchesse Anne	•							
Rennes: pl des Lices		•	•	•		•		
Retiers						•		
Sens de Bretagne	•							
Servon Vilaine							•	
St-Aubin Cormier			•					
St-Aubin d'Aubigné: pl du marché		•						

Location	M	T	W	Th	F	S	Su	Comments
St-Briac	•				•	•		Monday & Friday seasonal
St-Brice Coglès							•	2nd Sunday
St-Domineuc					•			
St-Georges de Reintembault			•					
St-Gilles					•			
St-Grégoire			•					
St-Lunaire							•	April to September
St-Malo: pl de la Mairie	•	•	•	•	•	•		
St-Médard sur Ille					•			
St-Méen le Grand					•			
St-Méloir des Ondes: marché aux Cadrans			•					
St-Ouen des Alleux		•						
Thorigné Fouillard						•		
Tinténiac			•					
Trans			•					
Vern sur Seiche					•			
Vitré: centre historique de Vitre	•							

Department of Morbihan

Location	M	T	W	Th	F	S	Su	Comments
Ambon							•	July & August
Arradon		•			•			
Arzon		•						
Auray: centre ville	•							
Baden							•	
Baud			•			•		1st Wednesday
Béganne							•	
Bubry			•					2nd & 4th Wednesday evenings
Carentoir		•						1st Tuesday
Carnac			•			•		
Caudan		•						
Cléguérec			•					Wednesday evening July & August
Crac'h				•				
Damgan		•				•		Saturday July to August
Elven				•				
Erdeven	•							Monday evening July to August
Étel		•						
Gourin: centre ville	•							
Grandchamp					•			1st Friday
Guéméne sur Scorff				•				
Guer		•						
Guidel					•		•	Evening July & August
Guilliers		•						
Hennebont				•				
Ile aux Moines					•			
Josselin						•		
Kervoyal			•					July & August
La Gacilly						•		
La Roche Bernard				•				
La Trinité Porhöet	•							2nd Monday

Location	M	T	W	Th	F	S	Su	Comments
La Trinité sur Mer		•		•				
Lanester		•						
Languidic				•				
Larmor Baden							•	
Larmor Plage		•					•	Tuesday evening
Le Bono					•			
Le Faourët			•					1st & 3rd Wednesday
Le Palais		•		•				
Le Roc St-André							•	
Locmaria							•	
Locmariaquer		•		•				
Locminé			•					
Locmiquélic				•				
Lorient			•	•				
Malansac		•						
Malestroit			•					
Mauron					•			1st & 3rd Friday
Muzillac					•		•	
Noyal							•	
Penestin			•				•	Wednesday July to August
Plescop						•	•	
Ploemeur			•				•	Wednesday evening July & August
Ploeren							•	
Ploërmel	•			•				
Plouay: pl de la Mairie						•		
Plougoumelen				•				
Plouhinec							•	
Pluvinger		•						2nd Tuesday
Pont Scorff					•			
Pontivy: pl Leperoit	•							
Port Crouesty	•							July & August
Port Louis		•			•			Tuesday evening including handicrafts
Port Navalo				•				July & August
Questembert: centre ville	•							
Quéven							•	
Quiberon					•			
Riantec		•						
Sarzeau			•					
Sauzon			•					
Sené				•				
Sérent		•						
St-Av							•	
St-Gildas de Rhuys							•	
St-Jean Brévelay		•						1st & 3rd Tuesday
St-Philibert				•				
St-Pierre Quiberon			•					
St-Servant Surzur							•	
Ste-Anne d'Auray		•						
Theix							•	
Vannes		•				•	•	

DEPARTMENTS

Cher	(18)
Eure et Loir	(28)
Indre	(36)
Indre et Loir	(37)
Loir et Cher	(41)
Loiret	(45)

Department of Cher								
Location	M	T	W	Th	F	S	Su	Comments
Argent sur Sauldre: pl du marché		•						
Aubigny sur Nère					•			
Avord			•					
Baugy				•				
Beffes		•						
Blet			•					
Bourges: Aéroport		•						
Bourges: Asnières	•							
Bourges: Chancellerie			•					
Bourges: Gibjoncs				•				
Bourges: Halle					•			
Bourges: marché couvert							•	
Bourges: Nation					•			
Bourges: pl des Marronniers				•				
Brinon sur Sauldre	•							3rd Monday
Chalivoy Milon				•				
Charenton du Cher		•						
Chârost				•				
Châteaumeillant				•				
Châteauneuf sur Cher					•			
Chezal Benoît				•				
Culan: pl du Champ de foire		•			•			
Dun sur Auron					•			
Foëcy				•				
Graçay				•				
Henrichemont			•					
Ids St-Roch					•			
Jouet sur l'Aubois	•							
La Chapelle d'Angillon				•				
La Guerche sur l'Aubois: pl C. de Gaulle		•						
Le Châtelet				•				

Location	M	T	W	Th	F	S	Su	Comments
Léré						•		
Les Aix d'Angillon		•						
Levet					•			
Lignières	•							
Lunery			•					
Mareuil sur Arnon			•					
Marmagne					•			
Marseille lès Aubigny			•					
Massay			•					
Mehun sur Yèvre			•					
Nérondes						•		
Neuvy sur Barangeon		•						
Orval					•			
Ourouer les Bourdelins				•				
Plaimpied Givaudins						•		
Préveranges	•							
Sancergues			•					
Sancerre		•				•		
Sancoins			•					
Saulzais le Potier				•				
Savigny en Sancerre				•				
Sens eaujeu	•							
St-Amand Montrond			•			•		
St-Doulchard		•						
St-Florent sur Cher						•		
St-Germain du Puy				•				
St-Satur				•				
Torteron							•	
Vailly sur Sauldre				•				
Vallenay				•				
Veaugues				•				
Vesdun			•					
Vierzon: cité Henri Sellier		•	•			•	•	

Department of Eure et Loire

Location	M	T	W	Th	F	S	Su	Comments
Auneau: centre ville					•			
Authon de perche: pl du marché		•			•			
Bonneval	•							
Brezolles				•				
Brou			•					
Chartres: bd de la Poste						•		All day
Chartres: pl Billard						•		
Chartres: pl du Cygne						•		All day
Châteaudun: pl du Gigne		•		•		•		Tuesday all day
Châteauneuf en Thymerais			•					
Cloyes sur le Loir						•		
Courville sur Eure				•				
Dreux: pl du marché couvert	•							All day
Epernon: pl Aristide Briand		•				•		

Location	M	T	W	Th	F	S	Su	Comments
Illiers					●			
Janville		●						
La Bazoche Gouet						●		
La Ferté Vidame				●			●	
La Loupe		●						
Lucé			●				●	
Luisant							●	
Maintenon				●				
Mainvilliers				●				
Morancez							●	
Nogent le Roi					●			
Nogent le Rotrou					●			All day
Senonches				●				
St-Denis des ponts							●	
St-Rémy sur Avre					●			
Vernouillet					●			
Voves: pl Mounowey		●						

Department of Indre

Location	M	T	W	Th	F	S	Su	Comments
Ardentes: pl St-Martin				●				
Argenton sur Creuse				●	●			
Azay le Ferron			●					Afternoon
Bélâbre				●				
Buzançais				●				
Chabris						●		
Chassignolles			●					Every two weeks
Châteauroux: pl Voltaire					●			
Châtillon sur Indre				●				
Châtillon sur Indre: pl du marche				●				
Clion sur Indre			●					
Déols		●		●				
Écueillé			●					2nd & 4th Wednesday
Éguzon Chantome			●					Every two weeks
Issoudun					●	●		Saturday all day
Le Blanc			●		●			
Le Châtre						●		All day
Levroux	●							All day
Lourddouiex St-Michel				●				Every two weeks
Luant			●					
Luçay le Mâle					●			Afternoon
Lureuil					●			Every two weeks
Meobeq				●				Afternoon 2nd Thursdays
Mézières en Brenne				●				
Orsennes			●					Every two weeks
Palluau: pl des Marroniers							●	
Pellevoisin: pl de la Mairie		●						
Reuilly				●				
St-Août: pl du Champ de foire		●						
St-Benoit du Sault						●		

Location	M	T	W	Th	F	S	Su	Comments
St-Denis de Jouhet		•						
St-Gaultier				•				
St-Genou					•			
Ste-Sévère			•					
Tournon St-Martin: Champ de Foire		•			•			
Valençay: pl de la Halles		•						
Vatan			•					
Vigoulant		•						Every two weeks
Vijon	•	•						Alternate Tuesday
Villedieu sur Indre			•					

Department of Indre et Loir

Location	M	T	W	Th	F	S	Su	Comments
Abilly		•		•	•			
Amboise: pl du Marché					•		•	
Autrèche		•						
Avoine: pl de l'Eglise				•				
Azay le Rideau			•					
Azay sur Cher				•			•	
Ballan Miré: pl de la Mairie				•	•		•	
Barrou				•				
Beaumont en Véron			•				•	
Bléré		•			•			Friday evening
Bossay sur Claise				•				
Bossée							•	
Bourgueil		•			•			
Chambray lès Tours				•			•	
Champigny sur Veude					•			
Charentilly		•		•				
Château la Vallière: pl du Champ Foire	•							
Château Renault: pl Jean Jaures		•			•			
Cheillé					•			
Chinon				•	•		•	
Chouzé sur Loire				•			•	
Cinq Mars la Pile			•					
Cléré les Pins			•					
Cormery			•					
Dame Marie les Bois			•					
Descartes				•			•	
Epeigneé les Bois							•	
Esves le Moutier			•					
Esvres sur Indre					•			
Ferrière Larçon			•					
Fondettes		•					•	
Genillé					•		•	
Gizeux			•					
Huismes		•						
Joué lès Tours		•	•		•		•	
L' Île Bouchard: pl Bouchard		•						
La Celle St-Avant			•					

Location	M	T	W	Th	F	S	Su	Comments
La Croix en Touraine				•				
La Membrolle sur Choisille		•						
La Riche			•		•			
La Ville aux Dames				•				
Langeais			•				•	
Le Grand Pressigny				•				
Ligueil: pl du G.Leclerc	•							
Limeray				•				
Loches			•	•	•			
Lussault sur Loire		•						
Luynes					•			
Manthelan				•				
Marigny Marmande	•							
Monnaie		•						
Montbazon		•			•			
Montlouis sur Loire			•				•	
Montrésor					•			
Monts					•			
Mosnes					•			
Nazelles Négron			•					
Neuil							•	2nd Sunday in December
Neuillé Pont Pierre		•						
Neuilly le Brignon			•					
Neuvy le Roi					•			
Notre Dame d'Oé			•					
Nouâtre					•			
Nouzilly					•			
Parcay Meslay					•			
Perusson							•	
Ports sur Vienne			•					
Preuilly sur Claise				•	•			
Restiné			•					
Reugny					•			14.00 to 18.00
Richelieu: pl du marché	•				•			1st & 3rd Monday
Savigné sur Lathan			•					
Savigny en Véron					•			
Savonnières					•		•	1st Friday
Sepmes					•			
Sorigny							•	
St-Aubin le Dépeint			•					
St-avrtin		•			•			
St-Branchs			•					
St-Cyr sur Loire: pl du C.Mailloux		•		•				
St-Flovier		•						
St-Laurent de Lin					•			
St-Martin le Beau		•						
St-Nicolas de Bourgueil			•					
St-Nicolas des Motets	•	•	•	•	•	•	•	
St-Paterne Racan			•					
St-Pierre des Corps		•	•		•			
St-Senoch			•					

Location	M	T	W	Th	F	S	Su	Comments
Ste-Maure de Touraine					•			
Tours: Beaujardin		•			•			
Tours: Beffroi			•					
Tours: Carreau des Halles		•			•			
Tours: Douets				•				
Tours: Francois Coppée					•			
Tours: Les Fontaines		•						
Tours: Maine							•	
Tours: Paul Bert		•						
Tours: pl St-Pierre				•				
Tours: Président Coty		•			•			
Tours: Rabelais							•	
Tours: St-Paul		•		•				
Tours: Strasbourg			•					
Tours: Velpeau			•				•	Friday evening
Tours: ZC Rives du Cher				•				
Truyes							•	
Veigné				•				
Véretz				•				
Vernou sur Brenne			•					
Villeperdue			•					
Vouvray		•		•				
Yzeures sur Creuse		•		•	•			

Department of Loir et Cher

Location	M	T	W	Th	F	S	Su	Comments
Blois: av de l'Europe							•	
Blois: pl Louis X11		•						
Blois: Pl Louis x11 et rue Châteaubriand			•					
Blois: qrt République					•			Evening
Blois: rue P et M Curie			•					
Bracieux			•					
Châtres sur Cher		•						
Contres					•			All day
Cour Cheverny		•						Afternoon
Droué							•	1st Sunday
Gièvres		•						
Herbault: pl du marché	•							
La Ferté St-Cyr			•					
Lamotte Beuvron				•				
Langon				•				
Marchenoir		•						
Mennetou sur Cher				•				
Mer				•				Evening
Mondoubleau: pl de la Mairie	•							Monday all day
Mont près Chambord		•						
Monthou sur Cher			•					
Montoire sur le Loir			•			•		Wednesday afternoon
Montrichard: centre ville	•				•			Monday afternoon. Friday pl de Verdun
Neung sur Beuvron							•	

Location	M	T	W	Th	F	S	Su	Comments
Nouan le Fuzelier			•					
Noyers sur Cher							•	
Onzain			•					Thursday afternoon
Oucques			•					
Ouzouer le Marché					•			
Romorantin Lanthenay			•		•			Wednesday all day
Salbris				•		•		
Savigny sur Braye		•						
Selles sur Cher				•				Thursday all day
St-Aignan						•		Saturday all day
St-Egrève: Mail Pierre Mendès France			•					
St-Egrève: pl Pompée			•		•			
St-Georges sur Cher					•			
St-Gervais la Fôret				•				
St-Laurent Nouan				•				
St-Martin d'Hères: pl de laRépublique				•			•	
St-Martin d'Hères: pl P.Eluard	•			•				
St-Martin d'Hères: rue G.Lorca			•		•			
Vendôme: centre ville				•				Friday all day
Vendôme: qtr des Rottes							•	
Villefranche sur Cher				•				

Department of Loiret

Location	M	T	W	Th	F	S	Su	Comments
Amilly: pl de l'Eglise							•	
Arthenay			•					
Beaugency						•		
Beaulieu sur Loire		•						
Beaune la Rolande		•						Afternoon from 13.00 to 18.00
Bellegarde: pl du centre ville	•							All day
Boiscommun				•			•	
Bonny sur Loire					•			
Briare				•				
Cepoy		•						
Chaingy							•	
Châlette sur Loing		•		•				
Châteauneuf sur Loire				•				Friday all day
Châteaurenard		•						
Châtillon Coligny				•				
Chécy						•		
Corbeilles en Gatinais				•				
Coullons				•				
Courtenay				•				
Dordives				•				
Fay aux Loges		•						
Ferrières en Gatinais				•				
Fleury les Aubrais		•						
Gidy							•	
Gien: pl de la Victoire					•			
Gien: pl St-Jaures		•						

Location	M	T	W	Th	F	S	Su	Comments
Huisseau sur Mauves					•			
Jargeau			•					
La Chapelle St-Mesmin							•	
La Ferté St-Aubin				•				
La Neuville sur Essone					•			
La Selle sur le Bied				•				
Ladon							•	
Lorris				•				
Malesherbes			•				•	Wednesday all day
Mardie							•	
Messas			•					
Meung sur Loire				•			•	Thursday afternoon 14.00 to 18.00
Montargis: marché couvert			•			•		
Montargis: pl de la République						•		
Montargis: pl Girodet			•			•		Saturday all day
Neuville aux Bois	•							
Nogent sur Vernisson				•				
Olivet					•			Evening
Orleans: Argonne					•			
Orleans: Dauphine		•						
Orleans: Halles de la Charpenterie						•		
Orleans: Münster rue Émile Zola			•					
Orleans: pl de la Bascule					•			
Orleans: pl Dunois				•				
Orleans: qrt de la Madeleine							•	
Orleans: qrt des Blossières		•						
Orleans: qrt la Source				•		•		
Orleans: St-Marceau rue Eugène Turbat				•				
Ouzouer sur Loire							•	
Ouzouer sur Trézée							•	
Pannes							•	
Patay		•				•		Tuesday afternoon 13.30 to 17.30
Pithiviers			•			•		Saturday all day
Puiseaux: pl du Jeu de Paume	•							
Saintay						•		
Sandillon							•	
Sermaises du Loiret				•				Thursday afternoon 14.00 to 19.00
St-Brisson						•		Saturday 14.00 to 18.00
St-Cyr en Val							•	
St-Denis de L'Hôtel							•	
St-Denis en Val							•	
St-Jean de Braye					•			Friday afternoon from 14.00 to 19.00
St-Jean de la Ruelle			•		•			Friday afternoon from 15.30 to 19.00
St-Jean le Blanc						•	•	Saturday 9.00 to 19.00
St-Pryvé St-Mesmin				•				
Sully sur Loire: bd Jeanne d'Arc	•							All day
Trainou		•						
Varennes Changy							•	
Villemandeur		•						

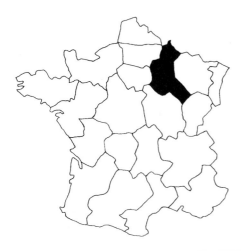

DEPARTMENTS

Ardennes	(8)
Aube	(10)
Marne	(51)
Haute Marne	(52)

Department of Ardennes

Location	M	T	W	Th	F	S	Su	Comments
Charleville Mézières: pl de l'Hotel de Ville			•				•	
Charleville Mézières: pl Ducale		•		•	•			
Charleville Mézières: qrt de la Ronde Couture							•	
Fumay			•					morning only
Givet					•			morning only
Monthermé	•							
Mouzon							•	2nd & 4th Sunday
Nouzonville: pl Gambette	•							
Rethel				•				
Revin: parking du centre		•		•				
Rocroi: pl Aristide Briand		•						
Sedan			•		•			
Vouziers					•			

Department of Aube

Location	M	T	W	Th	F	S	Su	Comments
Aix en Othe: le Mairie			•		•			
Arcis sur Aube: pl de la République				•				
Bar sur Aube				•				
Bar sur Seine				•				
Brienne le Château				•				
Chaource	•							
Chavanges			•					2nd Wednesday
Ervy le Châtel				•				
Essoyes		•						2nd Tuesday
Estissac							•	
Les Riceys				•				2nd Thursday
Marigny le Châtel							•	
Méry sur Seine				•				
Mussy sur Seine			•					

Location	M	T	W	Th	F	S	Su	Comments
Nogent sur Seine			•		•			
Pâllis				•				
Plancy l'Abbaye		•						
Romilly sur Seine: rues G.Leclerc & Carnot	•			•	•			
St-André les Vergers					•			Evening
Ste-Savine		•			•		•	
Troyes		•	•	•	•	•	•	All day except Sunday
Vendeuvre sur Barse			•					
Villenauxe la Grande					•			

Department of Marne

Location	M	T	W	Th	F	S	Su	Comments
Ay Champagne: pl de la Mairie					•			
Châlons en Champagne			•			•	•	
Dormans					•			
Épernay: pl Auban-Moët							•	
Épernay: pl Huges Plomb		•		•	•			All day
Épernay: St-Thibault			•			•	•	3rd Sunday
Esternay		•						
Fère Champenoise			•					
Fismes					•			
Montmirail: rue Lucien Mathieu	•							
Reims: av de Laon	•							
Reims: bd Carteret				•				
Reims: bd Wilson					•			
Reims: espl P.Cézanne			•					
Reims: Jean Jaurés							•	
Reims: pl des Argonautes			•					
Reims: pl du Boulingrin			•		•			
Reims: pl Jean Moulin		•						
Reims: pl Luton				•				
Reims: pl St-Maurice		•						
Reims: rue de Louvois							•	
Reims: rue P. Taittinger					•			
Sermaize les Bains							•	
Sézanne					•			
Ste-Menehould: pl d'Austerlitz	•							
Suippes				•				
Vitry le François: pl de la Halle			•			•		Saturday all day

Department of Haute Marne							
Location	M	T	W	Th	F	S	Su	Comments
Andelot Blancheville				•				Evening
Arc en Barrois					•			
Bleurville						•		Organic produce 1st Saturday 15.00 to 19.00
Bourbonne les Bains: près de l' Église			•					
Chalindrey: centre ville				•				
Chaumont			•			•		All day
Doulevant le Château	•							
Joinville					•			
Langres: pl Jeanson					•			
Montier en Der					•			
Nogent en Bassigny		•			•			
St-Dizier: Petites Halles			•					All day
St-Dizier: place du 11 Novembre 1918						•		All day
St-Dizier: Vert-Bois				•			•	
Villiers le Sec						•		Truffles from October to December

Department of Doubs

Location	M	T	W	Th	F	S	Su	Comments
Amancey		•						4th Tuesday
Arc et Senans			•					4th Wednesday
Aroey		•						2nd Tuesday
Audincourt: Champ Montants			•					
Audincourt: des Forges				•				
Audincourt: pl du Marché			•		•	•		Friday afternoon
Audincourt: rue des Mines							•	Food market
Baume les Dames			•					
Belleherbe			•					2nd Thursday
Besançon: Battant						•		
Besançon: Chaprais		•						
Besançon: Epoisses						•		
Besançon: Ille de France				•		•		
Besançon: Jouffroy						•		
Besançon: marché couvert	•	•	•	•	•	•	•	All day
Besançon: Montrapon			•					
Besançon: Palente		•			•			
Besançon: pl Battant	•							2nd Monday
Besançon: pl de la Révolution		•			•	•		Saturday all day
Besançon: Planoise				•			•	
Besançon: Planoise Franche-Comté		•			•			
Besançon: St-Claude		•			•			
Béthoncourt: pl du Centre Commercial					•			
Colombier Fontaine			•					2nd Wednesday
Damprichard			•		•			
Exincourt					•			
Fesches le Châteaux					•			
Gilley					•			4th Friday April to December
Grand Charmont		•						
Hérimoncourt		•						
Hôpitaux Neufs			•					July & August

Location	M	T	W	Th	F	S	Su	Comments
L' Isle sur le Doubs	•				•			3rd Monday
Le Russey						•		
Levier			•					
Maîche			•		•			
Malbuisson	•							July & August
Mandeure					•			Saturday afternoon
Montbéliard: la petite Hollande		•						
Montbeliard: parking ancien Leclerc					•			
Montbéliard: pl du marché			•					
Montbéliard: qtr de la Chiffogne			•					
Montbeliard: rue Clémenceau			•					
Morteau: pl de l'Hotel de Ville		•			•			
Mouthe					•			May to October
Ornans		•						3rd Tuesday
Pierrefontaine les Varans			•					3rd Wednesday
Pont de Roide					•			Afternoon
Pontarlier				•	•			Thursday 7:00 to 16:00
Quingey	•							1st Monday
Rougemont					•			2nd & 4th Friday
Seloncourt					•			
Sochaux			•					
St-Hippolyte				•				4th Thursday
Ste-Suzanne					•			All day
Valentigney: pl de la République		•						
Vennes					•			2nd Friday
Villers le Lac			•					1st Wednesday
Voujeaucourt					•			Afternoon

Department of Jura

Location	M	T	W	Th	F	S	Su	Comments
Arbois: pl du Champ de Mars		•		•				1st Tuesday
Arinthod		•						
Beaufort					•			
Bletterans: pl du marché		•						1st & 3rd Tuesday
Champagnole		•				•		2nd Tuesday
Chaumergy				•				
Chaussin		•						4th Tuesday
Clairvaux les Lacs			•					3rd Wednesday July & August
Cousance						•		
Coussange	•							
Damparis		•			•			
Dôle: pl Nationale		•		•		•		
Fraisans			•					1st Wednesday
Les Rousses				•				
Lons le Saunier				•		•		Thursday all day
Mignovillard			•					2nd Wednesday
Moirans en Montagne				•				
Morez						•		
Nozeroy	•							1st Monday
Orgelet			•					2nd Wednesday

Location	M	T	W	Th	F	S	Su	Comments
Poligny	•			•				2nd & 4th Monday
Salins les Bains	•		•			•		3rd Monday
Sellières			•					
St-Amour					•			
St-Aubin			•					
St-Claude			•		•			
St-Lupicin			•					
Tavaux					•			
Tavaux: Cité			•					

Department of Haute Saône

Location	M	T	W	Th	F	S	Su	Comments
Aillevillers		•						
Armance		•						3rd Tuesday
Baulay		•						1st Tuesday
Champagney				•				Last Thursday
Champlitte			•					1st Wednesday
Combeaufontaine		•						2nd Tuesday
Confians sur Lanterne		•						2nd Tuesday
Coravilliers				•				2nd Thursday
Dampierre sur Salon						•		1st Saturday
Faucogney				•				1st & 3rd Thursday
Favrney			•					2nd Wednesday March to October then 1st Wednesday
Fougerolles					•			
Fresse	•							Last Monday
Gevigney et Mercey					•			2nd & 4th Friday
Granges le Bourg	•							2nd Monday
Gray		•	•		•			2nd Wednesday
Gy		•						2nd Tuesday
Héricourt			•			•		Saturday evening
Jussey		•						
Lure		•						
Luxeuil les Bains						•		
Mélisey			•					
Noidans le Ferroux					•			2nd Friday
Norroy le Bourg					•			4th Friday
Pesmes		•						1st Tuesday
Plancher Bas				•				2nd Thursday
Plancher les Mines					•			
Porgerot		•						
Port sur Saône		•						
Ronchamp						•		
Saulnot			•					Last Wednesday
Scey sur Saône	•							2nd Monday
Servane	•							1st & 3rd Monday
St-Loup sur Semouse: pl Jean Jaures	•							
St-Sauveur							•	1st Sunday August to September 3rd Sunday October to May
Vauvilliers				•				2nd Thursday

Location	M	T	W	Th	F	S	Su	Comments
Vesoul			•		•			Smaller market Saturday
Villersexel			•					1st & 3rd Wednesday
Vitrey sur Mance			•					1st Wednesday

Department of Territoire de Belfort

Location	M	T	W	Th	F	S	Su	Comments
Beaucourt				•				
Belfort: Centre ville			•		•			
Belfort: marché des Vosges		•	•				•	
Belfort: Résidences			•					
Delle			•		•			
Giromagny					•			
Grandvillars					•			Afternoon
Morvillars		•						
Valdoie					•			

DEPARTMENTS

Aude	(11)
Gard	(30)
Hérault	(34)
Lozére	(48)
Pyrénées Orientales	(66)

Department of Aude								
Location	M	T	W	Th	F	S	Su	Comments
Azille						•		
Belpech			•					
Belveze du Razes		•				•		
Bize Minervois			•					
Bram			•					
Carcassonne		•		•		•		
Castelnaudary: pl de la République	•							All day
Caunes Minervois		•		•		•		
Chalabre						•		
Couiza		•				•		
Coursan	•	•	•	•	•	•		
Esperaza			•				•	
Fabrezan		•		•	•			
Fanjeaux						•		
Ferrals les Corbieres		•			•			
Gruissan: pl G.Leclerc & Bonance	•		•			•		
La Franqui	•			•				15th June to 15th September
La Palme		•			•			
La Redorte		•			•			
Leucate: Plage			•			•		15th June to 15th September
Leucate: Ville		•			•		•	
Lézignan Corbières			•					
Limoux		•			•			Tuesday evening July to August
Montolieu							•	Books & local produce each 3rd Sunday
Narbonne: Cours Mirabeau et Barques							•	
Narbonne: pl St-Paul			•					Food
Narbonne: pl Voltaire			•					Crafts & bric-a-brac
Narbonne: que Vallierè			•					Flowers
Narbonne: rue de la Parerie		•						
Port la Nouvelle			•			•		
Quillan			•			•		

Location	M	T	W	Th	F	S	Su	Comments
Rieux Minervois		•		•		•		
Saissac				•			•	July & August Thursdays in winter
Sigean: pl de la Libération		•			•			
St-Pierre la Mer	•	•	•	•	•	•	•	15th June to 15th September
Trebes			•					
Tuchan		•		•		•		

Department of Gard

Location	M	T	W	Th	F	S	Su	Comments
Aigues Mortes: av Frédéric Mistral			•				•	
Aimargues		•			•		•	
Alès: pl St-Jean	•	•	•	•	•	•		All day
Anduze: pl couverte, de la République			•					
Aramon			•					
Bagnols sur Cèze			•					
Barjac: pl Charles Guynel				•				
Beaucaire			•				•	
Bellegarde					•			
Bessèges			•					
Bréau et Salagosse							•	July & August
Chamborigaud					•			
Fourges			•					
Gagnières			•					
Génolhac		•			•			
Goudargues			•					
La Grande'Combe			•		•			
Lasalle	•			•				
Laudun	•							
Le Grau du Roi		•	•	•	•	•		
Le Vigan					•			
Marguerittes					•			
Méjannes le Clap	•							June to September
Meynes			•					
Molières sur Cèze					•		•	
Montfrin: centre ville		•						
Nimês: bd Jean Jaurès	•			•				
Orsan			•					
Pont St-Esprit					•			
Quissac		•						
ReMoulins				•				
Roquemaure		•						
Sauve				•	•			
Sommières		•			•			
Soudorgues							•	July & August
St-Ambroix: pl de l'Esplanade		•						
St-André de Valborgne					•			
St-Chaptes				•				
St-Gilles				•			•	
St-Hippolyte du Fort: pl des Casernes		•			•			
St-Jean du Gard: centre ville		•						

Location	M	T	W	Th	F	S	Su	Comments
St-Laurent d'Aigouze	•				•			
Sumène			•					
Tavl		•						
Uzès						•		
Valleraugue			•			•		seasonal
Vauvert			•			•		
Vergèze	•			•				
Villeneuve lès Avignon				•				

Department of Hérault

Location	M	T	W	Th	F	S	Su	Comments
Addissan		•			•			
Agde: centre ville			•					
Agde: la Tamarissiere	•	•	•	•	•	•	•	Food market in season
Agde: pl Gambetta			•					Food
Agde: pl Jean			•					Flowers
Alignan du Vent: rue de la République					•			
Aniane: pl de la Liberté			•					
Aspiran	•		•					
Autignac		•		•	•			
Baillargues: rue du Jeu de Ballon		•			•			
Balaruc les Bains: pl du marché		•			•			
Bassan		•			•			
Beaulieu			•		•			
Bedarieux: pl A.Thomas	•							
Bedarieux: pl de la Vierge	•							
Bessan: pl de la Promenade		•					•	
Béziers: allées Paul Riquet					•			All day
Béziers: pl David d'Angers					•			
Béziers: pl du 14 Juillet					•			
Boujan sur Libron: esplanade de la Mairie			•					
Candillargues: pl du Château				•				
Canet: pl du Village		•		•				October to June
Capestang: pl Jean Jaurès			•				•	
Carnon: centre administratif		•		•		•		June to September
Castelnau le Lez: pl du marché		•			•			
Castries: pl des Libertés				•				
Castries: pl du Cartel		•						
Caux: pl Publique				•				
Cazouls lès Béziers: pl de la Mairie		•		•	•			
Ceilhes et Rocozels			•				•	seasonal
Cers		•		•	•			
Cessenon sur Orb: pl Jean Moulin		•						
Claret: pl de l' Hermet			•					
Clermont L'Hérault			•			•		
Cournonterral: Viala et rue de la Chapelle			•			•		
Creissan		•						
Cruzy: pl Jean Jaures		•			•			
Ferrals les Montagne							•	Rural market during July & August
Florensac: pl de la République	•							Clothes

Location	M	T	W	Th	F	S	Su	Comments
Florensac: pl du marché					•			
Frontignan: La Peyrade	•							
Frontignan: pl de la Mairie				•	•			
Frontignan: pl Vauban	•							
Gabian			•		•			
Ganges: pl des Halles					•			
Ganges: plan de l' Ormeau		•						
Gigean: au jardin public		•						
Gignac: esplanade et Jeu Ballon						•		
Grabels: pl des Ecoles			•					
Graissessac: pl Gambette			•					
Grau d' Agde: parking au Front de Mer			•					
Grau d' Agde: pl de la République	•	•	•	•	•	•	•	Food market in season
Jacou							•	Small market
Juvignac: pl de la Lavande		•		•				
La Grande Motte: pl de la Mairie				•			•	June to September
La Salvetat sur Agout: esp. des Troubadours				•			•	Large market on the 19th
Lamalou les Bains: pl du marché		•						
Lansargues: pl St-Jean		•		•				
Laroque							•	seasonal
Lattes: centre			•					
Lattes: esplanade d'Aragon							•	
Laurens: pl du marché				•				
Le Cap d' Agde: Avant Port		•						Food
Le Cap d' Agde: Bulle d' Accueil			•					Local produce
Le Cap d' Agde: Ile des Loisirs			•					
Le Cap d' Agde: Mail de Rochelongue	•							
Le Cap d' Agde: parking du Gevaudan						•		seasonal
Le Cap d' Agde: pl du Barbeque		•				•		Tuesday local produce. Saturday seasonal
Le Caylar en Larzac: pl du village							•	
Le Puech		•	•		•			
Le Triadou							•	
Lespignan	•		•		•			
Lieuran les Béziers		•	•					
Lodève: centre ville						•		
Lodève: pl du marché	•							Local produce afternoons 16.30 to 19.30
Lunel Viel: pl du 14 Juillet						•		
Lunel: esplanade Roger Damour			•				•	Flowers on Sunday
Magalas		•						
Maraussan: pl du 14 Juillet		•			•			
Marseillan Plage	•	•	•	•	•	•		
Marseillan: pl de l' Église		•						
Marsillargues: sur les boulevards		•		•				
Mauguio: bvd de la Démocratie							•	
Mauguio: pl de la Libération		•		•				
Maureilhan			•		•			
Mèze: Esplanade			•				•	Also Thursday evening the port 20.00 to 24.00
Mireval: pl Louis d' Aragon		•		•				
Mons la Trivalle			•					seasonal
Montady: av des Platanes	•							
Montagnac: Esplanade					•			

Location	M	T	W	Th	F	S	Su	Comments
Montarnaud: av de Montpellier					•			
Montblanc: pl du Jeu de Paume	•		•		•			
Montpellier: Antigone			•					
Montpellier: av Samuel Champlin							•	Rural market
Montpellier: des halles Castellanes	•	•	•	•	•	•		
Montpellier: espace Mosson	•						•	Monday all day Sunday Antique, Bric-a-Brac etc
Montpellier: pl de la Comedie	•	•	•	•	•	•		
Montpellier: pl des Arceaux	•	•	•	•	•	•		
Montpellier: plan Cabanes et la Paillade	•	•	•	•	•	•	•	
Montpellier: rue des Etuves						•		3rd Saturday entertainments market
Montpeyroux			•					
Mudaison: pl Camille Reboul			•		•			
Murviel lès Béziers: esplanade des Tilleuls		•		•	•			
Nissan lez Enserune: pl du marché		•		•	•			
Octon				•				seasonal
Olargues: av de la Gare							•	
Olonzac: de la Promenade		•						
Palavas les Flots: parking des arènes marketl	•					•	•	Saturday flowers & bric-a-brac. Sunday large
Palavas les Flots: rue Maguelone				•				
Palavas les Flots: rue St-Roch			•					
Paulhan: bd de la Liberté				•				
Perols: pl Carnot	•							
Pézenas: cours Jean Jaures					•			
Pinet		•						
Pomérols: pl du Jeu de Ballon	•			•				
Portiragnes							•	Evening craft markets in season
Portiragnes: plage Front de Mer		•			•			
Portiragnes: plage parking Tramontane	•							
Portiragnes: tour du guet		•						
Portiragnes: ville rue de la Mairie				•				
Poussan: pl du marché		•			•			
Pouzolles: pl du marché			•		•			
Prades le Lez: pl du marché	•							
Puimisson: Esplanade		•	•		•			
Puissalicon		•			•			All day
Puisserguier: pl de l' Église		•						
Puisserguier: Promenade					•			
Quarante: pl de l' Abbadié			•		•			
Roquebrun: pl du marché		•			•			
Salasc							•	seasonal
Saussan							•	Country market
Sauvian: pl du marché					•			
Serignan: allées de la République	•		•		•			
Servian: pl du marché		•		•		•		
Sète: av Victor Hugo					•			Regional produce
Sète: pl Aristide Briand			•					
Sète: pl Léon Blum			•					Flowers
Sète: rue Alsace Lorraine			•					Local produce
St-André de Sangonis: pl de la Mairie		•			•			
St-Aunes: pl du Foyer		•						

Location	M	T	W	Th	F	S	Su	Comments
St-Bauzille de Putois: pl du Christ			•					
St-Brès: pl de la Ramade		•			•			
St-Chinian: Promenade				•			•	
St-Clement de Riviere: centre du Boulidou				•			•	
St-Gély du Fesc: Le mail du Devois				•	•			
St-Geniès des Mourges: pl de l' Abbaye			•					
St-Georges d' Orques: pl du St-Georges			•		•			
St-Gervais sur Mare: pl de Quai			•					
St-Jean de Beuges				•				
St-Jean de Fos: pl de la Mairie		•						
St-Jean de Vedas: pl de l' Ortet					•			
St-Jean de Vedas: pl du Pradet				•				
St-Martin de Londres: pl du marché		•						
St-Mathieu de Tréviers				•				Afternoon
St-Nazaire de Ladarez: pl de l' Église				•				All day
St-Pargoire: pl Roger Salengro		•						
St-Pons de Thomieres: pl des Tilleuls			•					
St-Thibery: pl du marché		•						
Thézan lès Béziers: pl de la Mairie		•		•				
Tourbes: pl du Quai			•					
Vacquieres			•					
Valflaunès: pl du village							•	
Valras Plage: pl Charles de Gaulle	•				•			
Vendargues: parking Caussel							•	
Vendres: pl du village	•		•		•			During winter
Vendres: plage		•		•			•	seasonal
Vias			•			•		
Vic la Gardiole: bd des Aresquiers				•				
Villeneuve lès Beziers: pl de la Révolution		•			•	•		
Villeneuve les Maguelonne: pl de l' Église		•	•	•				
Villeveyrac		•		•				

Department of Lozére

Location	M	T	W	Th	F	S	Su	Comments
Aumont Aubrac					•			
Bagnols les Bains			•					
Barre des Cevennes					•			1st July to 15th September
Chambon le Château			•					
Chanac			•				•	
Châteauneuf de Randon	•							
Collet de Deze		•						
Fournels			•					1st & 3rd Wednesday
Ispagnac		•			•			
La Malene	•							June onwards depending on the season
Langogne		•			•			Evening July & August
Le Bleymard					•			
Le Chastel Nouvel						•		
Le Pompidou					•			25th June to 30th September
Le Pont de Montvert		•						1st June to 30th September
Le Rozier		•			•			

Location	M	T	W	Th	F	S	Su	Comments
Marvejols						•		Thursday evening markets at pl Chanelles
Mende		•				•		
Meyrueis		•				•		
Rieutort de Randon							•	
St-Chely d'Apcher				•				
St-Germain du Teil					•			
St-Privat de Vallongue							•	July & August
Ste-Croix Vallee Français							•	
Ste-Enimie		•				•		
Vialas		•			•			
Villefort	•							1st Monday in August

Department of Pyrénées Orientales

Location	M	T	W	Th	F	S	Su	Comments
Amélie les Bains: pl du marché	•	•	•	•	•	•	•	
Argelès sur Mer: plage bvd de la Mer	•	•	•	•	•	•	•	15th June to 31st August
Argelès sur Mer: village			•		•			
Arles sur Tech			•					
Bages		•			•			
Baho			•					
Baixas		•						
Banyuls sur Mer: rue du 14 Juillet				•			•	
Bolquère Pyrénées 2000	•							
Bompas			•					
Bouleternère	•	•	•	•	•	•	•	
Bourg Madame: pl Salvat				•				
Brouilla		•	•					
Cabestany			•					
Canet en Roussillon: Plage		•	•	•	•	•	•	
Canet en Roussillon: plage Canet sud	•							July & August
Canet en Roussillon: village			•		•			
Canohès: pl du Bicentenaire		•	•					
Caudiès de Fenouillèdes	•	•	•	•	•	•	•	
Cerbère		•		•				
Céret						•		
Claira			•	•				
Collioure			•				•	
Corneilla la Rivière			•	•				
Elne	•		•	•				
Espira de l'Agly	•			•				
Estagel: allée des Tilleuls	•			•				
Formigueres						•		
Ille sur Têt			•	•				
Le Barcarès: allée des Arts		•	•					Evening
Le Barcarès: Coudalère			•				•	Evening
Le Barcarès: pl du marché	•		•		•		•	Sunday Seasonal
Le Barcarès: pl du Tertre		•	•					15th June to 15th September
Le Boulou: pl de la Mairie			•					
Le Soler	•	•			•			
Les Angles: pl du marché		•						

Location	M	T	W	Th	F	S	Su	Comments
Maureillas las Illas		•		•				
Maury	•	•	•	•	•	•	•	
Millas		•		•				
Mont Louis		•		•				
Néfiach	•			•				
Olette et Evol				•				
Osséja: pl St-Pierre				•				
Palau del Vidre		•		•				
Perpignan: de la République	•	•	•	•	•	•	•	Monday food only
Perpignan: marché du Haut Vernet	•	•	•	•	•	•	•	
Perpignan: pl Cassanyes	•	•	•	•	•	•	•	
Perpignan: pl de Montbolo			•					
Perpignan: pl des Poilus	•	•	•	•	•	•	•	
Perpignan: pl Rigaud						•		Organic produce
Perpignan: St-Louis av Joffre	•	•	•	•	•	•	•	
Perpignan: St-Martin pl Vaillant Couturier			•		•			
Peyrestortes		•		•				
Pézilla la Rivière		•		•				
Pia				•				
Pollestres	•		•	•				
Ponteilla			•					
Port Vendres					•			
Prades		•						
Prats de Mollo la Preste			•	•				
Rivesaltes: allées Mal Joffre	•							
Saillagouse		•		•				
Salses			•					
Sorède		•		•				
St-André				•	•			
St-Cyprien: plage		•		•				seasonal
St-Cyprien: village			•					
St-Estève					•			
St-Féliu d'Avall	•			•				
St-Génis des Fontaines		•		•				
St-Jean pl de Corts	•	•						
St-Laurent de Cerdans						•		
St-Laurent de le Salanque			•				•	
St-Paul de Fenouillet			•		•			
Ste-Marie la Mer: plage		•		•				
Ste-Marie la Mer: village			•		•			
Thuir					•			
Torreilles		•			•			Friday seasonal
Toulouges: pl Louis Lacaze		•			•			
Trouillas		•	•	•				
Vernet les Bains: pl de la République	•		•		•			
Villelongue de la Salanque			•	•				
Villeneuve de la Raho			•					
Vinça		•		•				
Vingrau			•		•			

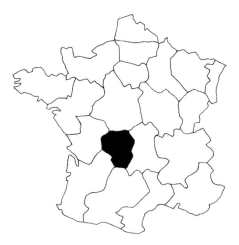

DEPARTMENTS

Corrèze	(19)
Creuse	(23)
Haute Vienne	(87)

Department of Corrèze

Location	M	T	W	Th	F	S	Su	Comments
Albussac							•	
Allassac: pl de la République				•				2nd & 4th Friday
Argentat			•					1st & 3rd Thursday
Arnac Pompadour					•			2nd & 4th Saturday
Aubazine		•					•	
Ayen		•						3rd Wednesday
Beaulieu sur Dordogne				•				1st & 3rd Friday
Beynat		•			•			3rd Wednesday
Bort les Orgues		•						2nd & 4th Tuesday
Bugeat			•					2nd & 4th Thursday
Chamberet				•				3rd Friday & 9th of the month
Chamboulive								2nd
Corrèze	•							3rd Monday
Donzenac			•				•	
Égletons							•	1st & 3rd Friday
Eygurande		•						2nd & 4th Wednesday
Goulles								24th
Juillac				•				1st & 3rd Friday
Lagraulière								10th
Larche			•					2nd Wednesday
Le Lonzac	•							2nd Monday
Lubersac			•					1st & 3rd Wednesday
Marcillac la Croisille			•					1st & 3rd Wednesday
Masseret								12th
Meilhards	•							1st Monday
Meymac					•			2nd & 4th Friday
Neuvic		•	•					1st & 3rd Tuesday
Objat		•						2nd, & 4th Tuesday
Peyrelevade								5th
Seilhac								25th
Sornac								2nd & 17th

Location	M	T	W	Th	F	S	Su	Comments
St-Augustin	•							1st Monday
St-Privat								15th & 28th except February when 24th
Treignac		•				•		6th & 22nd of the month
Tulle: marché couvert			•					2nd & 4th Wednesday
Tulle: marché de la Gare			•			•		1st & 3rd Wednesday
Tulle: pl Gambetta			•			•		
Tulle: pl Msg Berteaud			•			•		
Ussel			•			•		2nd & 4th Wednesday
Uzerche								20th

Department of Creuse

Location	M	T	W	Th	F	S	Su	Comments
Ahun:pl Dr.Coudère			•					
Aubusson				•				
Auzances: pl du marché		•						
Azerables								15th
Bellegarde en Marche								3rd
Bénévent l'Abbaye		•						
Bourganeuf			•					
Boussac				•				
Chambon sur Voueize			•					
Châtelus Malvaleix				•				
Cheniers								21st May & 25 th October
Crocq							•	1st & 3rd Sunday
Dun le Palestel				•				
Évaux les Bains: pl de la Poste	•							
Faux la Montagne	•							July & August
Felletin				•				
Genouillac		•						
Gentioux		•						1st Tuesday
Gouzon: pl du marché		•						
Grand Bourg								2nd & 17th
Guéret: pl Bonnyaud				•		•		
Jarnages				•				4th Thursday
La Courtine			•					2nd Wednesday
La Souterraine				•	•			
Mainsat			•					1st Wednesday
Mérinchal	•							1st Monday
Naillat							•	1st Sunday in August
Pontarion					•			1st Friday
Royère de Vasivière		•						July - August
Sardent					•			3rd Friday
Soumans			•					2nd Wednesday
St-Dizier Leyrenne				•				
St-Georges la Pouge		•						1st Tuesday
St-Maurice la Souterraine							•	3rd Sunday afternoon
St-Yrieix la Montagne								Farmers evening markets 28th June & 30th August
Vallière			•					2nd Thursday

Department of Haute Vienne

Location	M	T	W	Th	F	S	Su	Comments
Aixe sur Vienne						•		Fair 1st Friday
Bellac		•				•		Fair 1st monthly & 1st Thursday in September
Châlus				•				Fair 2nd Thursday
Châteauponsac							•	Fair 3rd of the month
Limoges: Cité Léon Jouhax				•				
Limoges: Landouge							•	Last Sunday
Limoges: pl Carnot	•	•	•	•	•	•	•	
Limoges: pl de la Motte	•	•	•	•	•	•	•	
Limoges: pl des Bancs		•				•		
Limoges: pl des Carmes		•				•		
Limoges: pl du Commerce				•				
Limoges: pl Haute Cité			•					
Limoges: pl Marceau						•		
Limoges: pl Paul Parbelle			•					
Limoges: rue Halévy		•						
Limoges: rue Jean Gabin				•				
St-Junien						•		Fair 3rd Saturday
St-Léonard de Noblat						•		
St-Yrieix la Perche					•			Fair 2nd & 4th Friday

DEPARTMENTS

Meurthe et Moselle	(54)
Meuse	(55)
Moselle	(57)
Vosges	(88)

Department of Meurthe et Moselle

Location	M	T	W	Th	F	S	Su	Comments
Auboué: pl Gal Leclerc				•				
Audan le Roman: pl de l' Hôtel de Ville			•					
Baccarat: pl du Gal Leclerc					•			
Badonviller: pl de la République				•				
Bayon: pl du Château			•					
Blainville sur L'Eau: pl du Lorraine		•						
Blâmont: pl du Général de Gaulle					•			Afternoon
Bouxières aux Dames					•			Afternoon
Bouxieres aux Dames: pl Clemenceau				•				Afternoon
Briey: pl de Niederaussem			•					
Chaligny: Parc Edmond Pintier							•	Organic produce 1st Sunday
Champigneulles: Esplanade F.			•		•			
Cirey sur Vézouze: pl Leclerc				•				
Clarieu					•			
Croismare: pl Stanislas							•	
Custines: pl de l' Église		•						
Dieulouard: pl du 8 Mai 45		•						
Dombasle				•				
Foug: pl Marbourg		•						
Frouard: pl Nationale							•	
Gerbéviller: pl de la Mortagne			•					
Gorcy: pl de l' Église	•							
Haroue: pl les Landres et Rues principales							•	Last Sunday
Herserange: pl Hôtel d' Ville			•					
Homécourt: pl du Gal Leclerc		•						
Hussigny-Godbrange				•				
Jarny: pl Génot					•			
Jarville la Malgrange: pl du Souvenir Francais				•				
Jaulny: pl de la Fontaine							•	March to November
Joeuf		•			•			
Labry			•					

Location	M	T	W	Th	F	S	Su	Comments
Laxou: pl du jet d'eau					●			
Liverdun: pl de la gare						●		
Longuyon: pl Hôtel de Ville					●		●	Sunday June
Longwy: pl Leclerc		●		●	●			
Ludres: pl Ferri de Ludres					●			
Lunéville		●		●	●			
Marbache: av Foch					●			
Maxeville: viaduct			●					
Mercy le Bas: pl de la Chapelle			●					
Mont Bonvillers: pl du Monument		●						
Mont St-Martin		●						Afternoon
Mont sur Meurhte			●					Afternoon
Moutiers			●					
Nancy: Beauregard					●			
Nancy: Haut du Lièvre: av Pinchard							●	
Nancy: Marché centrale		●	●	●	●	●		
Nancy: Marché d' Haussonville: pl L.Pelerin		●		●	●			
Nancy: pl Henri Mengin		●			●			All day
Nancy: Vieille Ville: rue de la Gendarmerie						●	●	2nd Saturday
Neuves Maisons: marché couvert					●			
Pagny sur Moselle: pl ChArles de Gaulle			●					
Piennes: pl Jean Jaurés			●					
Pompey: av Gambetta			●					
Pont à Mousson: pl St-Antione					●			
Pont St-Vincent: pl Roger Salengro				●				
Pulnoy: pl de le République							●	
Richardménil: pl du centre commercial				●				
Rosieres aux Salines: pl St-Pierre		●						
Saulxures les Nancy: parking municipal				●				
St-Nicholas de Port: rue Jolain				●				
Thiaucourt			●					
Tomblaine: av de Hasbergen	●						●	
Toul: Croix de Metz							●	
Toul: pl marché			●	●				
Trieux			●					
Tucquegnieux: pl A.Llamoine			●		●			Afternoons
Val et Chatillon					●			
Valleroy: pl Les Mêlées				●				
Vandoeuvre les Nancy: Haut du Lièvre							●	
Vandoeuvre les Nancy: pl de la République					●		●	Afternoons
Varangéville: rue Georges Toussaint			●					
Varny			●					
Villers les Nancy: Mail de Clairlieu							●	
Villerupt: Cantebonne			●					Afternoon
Villerupt: pl Jeanne d' Arc		●			●			
Villiers					●			

Department of Meuse

Location	M	T	W	Th	F	S	Su	Comments
Bar le Duc		•		•		•		Smaller market Thursday
Bar le Duc: Côte Ste-Catherine							•	
Bouligny			•					
Clermont en Argonne							•	Flowers
Commercy: pl Charles de Gaulle	•				•			
Damvillers						•		
Étain				•				Afternoon
Gondrecourt le Château				•				
Ligny en Barrois		•		•				
Montmédy		•						
Revigny sur Ornain			•			•		Smaller market Saturday
Spincourt		•						
St-Mihiel						•		
Stenay					•			
Tronville en Barrois				•				
Vaucouleurs						•		
Verdun		•		•				
Vignuelles les Hattonchatel						•	•	Saturday afternoon & Sunday July to August
Void Vacon				•				

Department of Moselle

Location	M	T	W	Th	F	S	Su	Comments
Albestroff						•		
Algrange				•				
Amnéville		•				•		
Ars sur Moselle: pl Roosevelt						•		April to September
Audun le Tiche			•			•		Saturday 14.00 to 19.00
Aumetz			•					
Ban St-Martin				•				
Behren lès Forbach						•		
Bitche		•				•		
Boulange		•						1st & 3rd Wednesday
Boulay				•				
Bouzonville		•						
Cattenom		•						Afternoon
Château Salins			•					Important market
Cité des Roses			•					
Clouange		•				•		Smaller market Friday
Courcelles Chaussy			•					Afternoon from 14.00 to 17.00
Créhange	•					•		1st Friday afternoon
Creutzwald			•					
Delme			•					
Dieuze				•				
Falck			•					
Fameck						•		
Farébersviller: pl du centre commercial			•		•			Friday afternoon
Faulquemont				•				
Fénétrange			•					

Location	M	T	W	Th	F	S	Su	Comments
Florange				•				
Folschviller					•			
Forbach: centre		•		•				
Freyming la Chapelle			•					Afternoon except 3rd Wednesday
Freyming Merlebach: av Erckmann Chatrian			•					3rd Wednesday afternoon
Freyming Merlebach: Cité la Chapelle			•					Afternoon except 3rd Wednesday
Freyming Merlebach: pl de Paris			•					Afternoon except 3rd Wednesday
Freyming Merlebach: rue du Maréchal Foch				•				
Gandrange			•					
Guenange: pl de la République	•							Afternoon
Guenange: pl St-Benoît						•		Afternoon
Hagondange: Cites	•							
Hagondange: pl Jean Burger					•			
Hayange: centre				•	•			
Hayange: Konacker				•				Afternoon from 14.00 to 18.00
Hettange Grande			•					
Hombourg Haut	•							
Knutange			•					
L' Hôpital					•			
Le Ban St-Martin: pl du Complexe Sportif					•			
Maizières lès Metz				•				
Marly: pl du General de Gaulle	•							
Merlebach				•				
Metz: av de Nancy			•		•			
Metz: Belle Croix				•				
Metz: pl Arsène Vigeant				•				Important market
Metz: pl Bouchotte		•						
Metz: pl d' Armes						•		October to April
Metz: pl de la Brigade d' Alsace				•				Important market
Metz: pl de la Cathédrale	•			•		•		
Metz: pl Durutte		•						
Metz: pl St-Jacques	•			•		•		Tuesday & Thursday from October to April
Metz: pl St-Livier		•						
Metz: rue Fort des Bordes	•				•			
Metzervisse	•							Until 15.00pm
Mondorff		•						
Montigny les Metz: pl de la Nation	•				•			
Montigny les Metz:pl des Vacons	•							
Morhange		•						
Moyeuvre Grande		•				•		
Moyeuvre: Cité Froidcul						•		Afternoon
Neufchef	•							
Nilvange					•			
Ottange				•				
Petite Rosselle: marché de Vieille Verrie			•	•				
Phalsbourg					•			
Plappeville	•							
Puttelange aux Lacs				•				Afternoon
Remilly		•						Afternoon
Rodemack	•							
Rombas: pl de l' Hôtel de Ville				•				

Location	M	T	W	Th	F	S	Su	Comments
Rombas: rue de Versailles				•				
Rosselange					•			Afternoon
Sarralbe				•				
Sarrebourg		•			•			
Sarreguemines: rue et Passage du Marché		•			•			
Sarreguemines: rue et Ruelle de l' Église		•			•			
Serémange Erzange			•					
Sierck les Bains			•					Afternoon
St-Avold		•			•			
Ste-Marie aux Chênes					•			
Stiring Wendel: centre ville				•		•		
Stiring Wendel: qrt Habsterdick				•				
Talange			•					
Terville					•			
Thionville: rue de Manège		•		•		•		
Uckange			•		•			
Vic sur Seille			•					2nd Wednesday
Vigy					•			2nd Friday afternoon
Volmerange les Mines			•					Afternoon
Woippy: pl Jean Perrin					•			Afternoon
Woustwiller			•					
Yutz					•			

Department of Vosges

Location	M	T	W	Th	F	S	Su	Comments
Anould			•					
Bains les Bains				•				
Ban de Lavline			•					Afternoon
Bruyères			•					
Bulgnéville				•				
Celles sur Plaine			•					
Charmes		•			•			2nd Tuesday from 16.00 to 20.00
Châtel sur Moselle					•			
Châtenois						•		Afternoon
Contrexéville: pl des Fontaines		•			•			
Corcieux	•							
Cornimont			•					
Darney					•			
Docelles	•							4th Monday
Éloyes							•	
Épinal			•	•		•		
Étival Clairefontaine			•					
Fontenay le Château		•						
Fraize					•			
Gérardmer				•		•		
Granges sur Vologne		•				•		
Gruay les Surance	•							2nd Monday
Hennezel			•					1st Wednesday
La Bresse							•	
Lamarche					•			

Location	M	T	W	Th	F	S	Su	Comments
Le Thillot						•		
Le Tholy	•							3rd Monday from May to October except July
Le Val d'Ajol							•	
Liffol le Grand				•				
Martigny les Bains					•			
Mirecourt				•		•		2nd & 4th Thursday
Monthureux sur Saône						•		
Moyenmoutier				•			•	Sunday April to September
Neufchâteau			•			•		
Neuveville sur Châtenois			•					
Nomexy						•		
Plainfaing							•	1st May to 31st August
Plombières		•			•			Monday in August
Portieux		•					•	1st Sunday after 10th
Pouxeux	•							3rd Monday
Rambervillers				•				
Raon l' Étape						•		
Remiremont		•			•			Friday fruit & vegetables
Rupt sur Moselle						•		Afternoon
Saulxures sur Moselotte			•					
Senones	•				•			
St-Dié		•			•	•		Saturday afternoon
St-Maurice sur Moselle							•	May to October
Tendon				•				2nd Thursday
Thaon les Vosges: centre ville				•				Large market 1st Thursday
Vagney	•							1st Monday
Vittel: pl Général de Gaulle			•			•	•	
Xertigny				•				

DEPARTMENTS

Ariège	(9)
Averyron	(12)
Haute Garonne	(31)
Gers	(32)
Lot	(46)
Hautes Pyrénées	(65)
Tarn	(81)
Tarn et Garonne	(82)

Department of Ariège

Location	M	T	W	Th	F	S	Su	Comments
Ax les Thermes; pl St-Jérome		•		•	•			15th June to 15th September
Castillon		•						Crafts & general markets
Daumazan sur Arize				•				
Foix	•				•			1st, 3rd & 5th Monday Cattle
La Bastide de Sérou				•				
La Tour du Crieu			•					
Laroque d`Olmes				•	•			
Lavlanet		•		•				
Le Carla Bayle							•	All day Sundays July & August
Le Fossat			•					3rd & 5th Wednesday
Le Mas d`Azil			•			•		Saturday cattle
Lézat sur Lèze					•			
Massat				•				2nd & 4th Thursday
Mazères				•				
Mirepoix: pl Phillipe de Levis	•			•		•		Thursday seasonal Saturdays April to September
Oust				•				
Pailhès							•	2nd & 5th Sundays
Pamiers; pl Jean Jaurès		•		•		•		
Quié							•	4th July to 29th August
Rouze				•				
Savrdun					•			Cattle & general market
Seix			•					2nd & 4th Wednesday 1st July to 15th Septemberl
St-Girons						•		Christmas market
St-Jean du Falga			•					
St-Paul de Jarrat					•			
St-Ybars			•					4th Wednesday
Tarascon sur Ariège			•			•		
Varilhes		•				•		2nd & 4th Tues, Cattle 1st & 3rd Tues. Cattle Saturdays.
Verniolle							•	

Department of Aveyron

Location	M	T	W	Th	F	S	Su	Comments
Aguessac							•	July & August
Alpuech	•	•	•	•	•	•	•	11th June to 6th October
Arvieu			•					1st Wed. Weekly in July & August for local produce
Aubin			•		•			
Baraqueville							•	15th June to 15th September. Local produce
Belmont							•	
Bozouls			•					
Brousse le Château		•						July & August
Camarès			•					July & August Fair 4th Wednesday
Canet de Salars				•				Thursday seasonal
Capdenac Gare		•			•			
Cassagnes Bégonhès				•				
Compeyre							•	June to September
Coupiac			•					Evening July & August
Cransac					•			Afternoon
Decazeville		•		•				
Durenque			•	•				Fair 1st Thursday, Market Wednesday after fair
Entraygues		•		•				Friday & Tues seasonal Wed evening local produce
Espalion		•		•				
Estaing			•					Evening 18.00 during season
Firmi					•			
Grand Vabre							•	July & August
La Couvertoirade			•				•	Sunday seasonal
La Fouillade					•			July & August Local produce
La Primaube							•	
La Salvetat Péyralès			•					1st Wednesday
Laguiole					•			1st May to 30th September
Laissac		•						
Lanuéjouls							•	
Marcillac Vallon							•	
Millau	•		•		•			Monday evening July to August
Montbazens			•					
Montredon du Larzac			•					July & August
Mostuéjouls					•			July & August Local produce
Mur de Barrez				•				Also Thursday evening for local produce
Najac							•	seasonal
Naucelle					•			July & August
Olemps				•				
Onet le Château					•			
Pont de Salars			•		•			Wednesday evening for local produce
Pradinas					•	•		Pottery last week-end in July
Réquista	•		•					Sheep Monday, 2nd Thursday
Rieupeyroux							•	16th June to 29th September Local produce
Rignac		•						
Rodez			•		•	•		Friday evening
Salles Curan		•			•			Tuesday evening July to August
Sauveterre de Rouergue				•				Evening 19.00 9th July to 20th August
Sévérac le Château				•	•			Friday evening local produce in July & August
St-Affrique				•		•		Thursday in July & August

Location	M	T	W	Th	F	S	Su	Comments
St-Amans des Cots				•				
St-Chély d'Aubrac		•					•	
St-Côme d'Olt							•	26th June to 4th September Local produce
St-Félix de Lunel								20th
St-Geniez d'Olt					•			Also Saturday evening during summer
St-Jean de Bruel			•				•	Gastronomic delicacies Sun morning July & August
St-Laurent d'Olt				•				Last Friday in July
St-Parthem			•					Evening 19.00 July & August Local produce
St-Rome de Tarn		•						12th July to 30th August Local produce
St-Saturnin de Lenne						•		4th Saturday in May
St-Sernin sur Rance			•					2nd Wed Evenings 18.00 July & August Local produce
Ste-Eulalie d'Olt							•	3rd Sunday in August
Ste-Geneviève			•					
Villecomtal			•					seasonal
Villefranche de Panat					•		•	July & August Except for the 4th week
Villefranche de Rouergue				•				
Villeneuve d'avyron							•	Local produce
Viviez					•			

Department of Haute Pyrénées

Location	M	T	W	Th	F	S	Su	Comments
Aspet			•			•	•	
Aurignac		•						
Auterive: pl de la Madeleine				•				
Bessières: pl du marché	•							
Boulogne sur Gesse			•					
Carbonne			•					
Cazères sur Garonne						•		Picturesque open air market
Cintegabelle			•					
Grenade						•		
L' Isle en Dodon						•		
Luchon			•			•		seasonal
Montastruc la Conseillère							•	
Montesquieu Volvestre		•				•		Alternate Tuesdays
Montgiscard							•	
Montréjeau	•							Ancient market every last Monday in July
Muret: secteur Nord		•				•	•	Flea market Sunday Secondhand books alternate Saturdays
Nailloux			•					
Plaisance du Touch				•		•		
Revel						•		Also livestock November to mid March
Rieumes			•					
Rieux Volvestre		•						1st Tuesday
St-Félix			•					
St-Gaudens				•		•		November to April
St-Martory					•			
Toulouse: Ancely						•		Friday 16.00 to 19.00
Toulouse: Arnaud Bernard		•	•	•	•	•	•	Secondhand books on Thursdays in July
Toulouse: Bellefontaine			•					
Toulouse: Carmes		•	•	•	•	•	•	

Location	M	T	W	Th	F	S	Su	Comments
Toulouse: d' Empalot			•					
Toulouse: de l'Ormeau		•			•			
Toulouse: de la pl Beteille		•	•	•	•	•	•	
Toulouse: de la pl St-Georges		•	•	•	•	•	•	
Toulouse: des Pradettes						•		Including organic produce
Toulouse: du bd de Strasbourg		•	•	•	•	•	•	
Toulouse: du Cristal Palace		•	•	•	•	•	•	
Toulouse: La Faourette		•				•		
Toulouse: pl du Capitole		•	•			•		Tuesday & Saturday Organic food
Toulouse: pl du marché aux Cochons		•	•	•	•	•	•	
Toulouse: pl du Ravlin						•		Small producers of food etc.
Toulouse: pl St-Aubin							•	
Toulouse: Rangueil			•				•	
Toulouse: Reynerie				•				
Toulouse: St-Cyprien		•	•	•	•	•	•	
Toulouse: St-Simon			•					
Toulouse: Victor Hugo		•	•	•	•	•	•	
Verfeil	•							
Villefranche de Lauragais					•			
Villemur sur Tarn						•	•	

Department of Gers

Location	M	T	W	Th	F	S	Su	Comments
Aignan: pl du Colonel Parisot	•							Also monday evening in July
Auch: pl de la Cathédrale				•		•		
Barbotan les Thermes			•					April to November
Bassoues							•	
Cazaubon					•			
Cologne	•			•				Monday evening from middle of July
Condom			•					
Eauze				•				
Fleurance: pl de la République			•	•				Tuesday all day
Gimont				•			•	seasonal
L' Isle Jourdain					•			
Lectoure				•				
Lombez					•			
Marciac			•					
Mauvezin: pl de la Libération	•			•				Friday evening July & August
Miélan				•				
Mirande: pl centrale de ville	•							
Montréal					•			
Nogaro			•			•		
Plaisance				•				
Riscle					•			
Samatan: pl du marché	•			•				Friday evening July & August
Saramon		•				•		
Seissan					•			
St-Clar				•				Evening July & August
Valence sur Baise			•					
Vic Fezensac			•		•			Wednesday evening

Department of Lot

Location	M	T	W	Th	F	S	Su	Comments
Arcambal							•	May to September
Assier	•							1st & 3rd Monday
Bagnac sur Célé			•					1st Wednesday
Beauregard		•		•	•			
Bétaille: Main square		•						Evening 17.00 to 20.00 local produce July & August
Biars sur Cère							•	
Brengues: Camping Municipal				•				Evening 17.00 to 21.00
Bretenoux		•			•			
Cahors: La Halle		•			•		•	All day covered market Sundays morning only
Cahors: pl Chapou			•		•			Evening July & August. Truffle markets from November to March
Cahors: Verrière de la Halle					•			November to March
Cajarc					•			Afternoon
Castelnau Montratier		•					•	2nd Tuesday
Catus		•						
Cazals			•				•	4th Wednesday
Concots			•				•	1st Wednesday
Douelle							•	
Duravl					•			
Espere							•	
Figeac		•		•				
Floirac		•			•			
Gourdon: pl St-Pierre		•		•	•			1st & 3rd Tuesday local produce Thursday seasonal
Gramat		•		•	•		•	2nd & 4th Thursday
Labastide Murat: pl de la Mairie			•	•			•	Sunday Seasonal Livestock 1st & 3rd Thursday 2nd & 4th Monday
Lacapelle Marival	•	•					•	Tuesday evening local produce 5.00 to 9.00, 2nd & 4th Monday
Lalbenque		•					•	Sunday local produce
Latronquière		•			•			2nd Friday
Le Vigan							•	
Leyme		•						4th Tuesday, Tuesday October to May
Limogne							•	
Livernon: Market place			•					Evening 17.00 to 20.00 local produce June to September
Luzech			•					1st Wednesday
Marcilhac sur Célé		•					•	July & August 1st Sunday
Martel		•			•			Truffles from December to January
Mercuès				•				
Miers: Main square					•			Evening 17.00 to 21.00 local produce
Montcuq: boulevard			•	•			•	2nd Wednesday, Thursdays, local produce July & August
Payrac		•						Local produce March to November
Pradines					•			
Prayssac: pl de la Liberté					•		•	Sunday for local produce
Puy L`Évêque		•			•			Evening August
Puybrun							•	

Location	M	T	W	Th	F	S	Su	Comments
Rocamadour								Evening July & August
Salviac		•			•			
Sauzet			•					
Souillac	•		•	•				July & August
Sousceyrac: pl du Foirail			•	•				2nd Wednesday Sunday local produce
St-Céré		•	•			•		1st & 3rd Wednesday
St-Cirq Lapopie			•					Wednesday June to September
St-Germain du Bel Air: Post office square					•		•	Local produce Seasonal on Sunday
St-Gery							•	April to September
St-Sozy					•			2nd Friday
Tauriac: pl de l'Église			•					Evening 17.30 to 20.30 July & August local produce
Thédirac							•	July & August
Vayrac				•		•		1st & 3rd Thursday

Department of Hautes Pyrénées

Location	M	T	W	Th	F	S	Su	Comments
Argelès Gazost: centre ville		•						All day
Arreau: pl de la Mairie			•					Very pretty market held all day
Arrens Marsous							•	seasonal
Bagnères de Bigorre						•		
Barèges			•					seasonal
Bordères Louron: pl de l' Église							•	
Campan			•					seasonal
Capvern les Bains: bvd des Pyrénées		•						April to October
Castelnau Magnoac: grand place						•		
Cauterets			•					seasonal
La Barthe de Neste							•	May to October
Lannemezan			•					Traditional market between 9.00 & 15.00
Loudenvielle		•						Evening
Lourdes: pl du Champ Commun	•	•	•	•		•	•	Thursday & Saturday all day
Loures Barousse					•			
Luz St-Sauveur: vieux qrt. De Luz	•							
Payolle					•			seasonal
Pierrefitte Nestalas						•		
Rabastens de Bigorre: pl centre ville	•							Livestock
Sarrancolin: pl de vivier		•			•			
St-Lary Soulan					•			
St-Pé de Bigorre			•					
Ste-Marie de Campan			•					seasonal
Tarbes: pl Marcadieu				•				
Tournay: la place		•						
Trie sur Baïse: le marché d'Europe		•						
Vic en Bigorre						•		
Vielle Aure		•						July & August

Department of Tarn								
Location	M	T	W	Th	F	S	Su	Comments
Albi: bvd de Strasbourg						•		
Albi: Halle de couvert		•	•	•	•	•	•	
Albi: la Cathédrale						•		Poultry market
Albi: pl Fernand-Pelloutier						•		
Albi: pl St-Salvy		•						Organic produce
Anglès			•					Last Thursday
Aussillon			•					
Cagnac les Mines			•					
Cahuzac sur Vère			•					
Carmaux					•			
Castres		•		•	•	•		Saturday at place Jean Jaurés
Cordes: pl de la Bouteillerie						•		
Gaillac					•			
Graulhet		•					•	
Labastide Rouairoux			•					
Labruguière				•				
Lacaune: pl Général de Gaulle							•	
Lautrec: central square				•				
Lavaur: Allées Jean Jaurés						•		Horses on 3rd Saturday
Lavaur: pl du Foirail						•		
Lisle sur Tarn: pl de la Mairie							•	2nd Sunday
Marssac			•					
Mazamet		•				•		Except public holidays
Monestiés							•	Food tasting local produce in July & August
Montredon Labessonnié			•			•		Saturday seasonal Food tasting
Murat sur Vèbre						•	•	
Pampelonne						•		
Puylaurens			•					
Rabastens						•		
Réalmont: pl de l' Église produce in July & August			•			•		Farm co-operative Friday taste home made
Réalmont: Salle Polyvalente			•					specialising in garlic & poultry
Roquecourbe				•				
Salvagnac			•					
St-Juéry				•				
St-Paul Cap de Joux		•						
St-Sulpice			•					
Trébas							•	Food tasting local produce in July & August
Vabre				•				

Department of Tarnet Garonne								
Location	**M**	**T**	**W**	**Th**	**F**	**S**	**Su**	**Comments**
Beaumont de Lomagne						•		
Castelsarrasin			•					
Caussade					•			
Caylus		•				•		Saturday seasonal
Finhan			•					
Grisolles			•					
Labastide St-Pierre			•					
Lafrançaise			•					
Laguépie		•						3rd Tuesday
Lauzerte						•		1st Monday
Lavit					•			
Moissac						•	•	
Monclar de Quercy				•				1st & 3rd Thursday
Montaigu de Quercy						•		
Montauban: pl Lulaque			•					
Montauban: pl Nationale	•	•	•	•	•	•	•	
Montauban: pl Prax Paris						•		
Montricoux					•			
Nègrepelisse		•						
Roquecor							•	
Septfonds			•					
St-Antonin Noble Val							•	
St-Nicolas de la Grav	•							
Valence d'Agen		•						
Verdun sur Garonne					•		•	
Vemille					•			

DEPARTMENTS

Nord	(59)
Pas de Calais	(62)

Department of Nord								
Location	M	T	W	Th	F	S	Su	Comments
Anzin: pl d'Anzin		•			•			
Arleux: rue des Murets		•						
Armentières: le Mairie					•			
Avsnes sur Helpe					•			
Bailleul: pl Ch de Gaulle		•						
Bavay					•			
Bergues: pl de la République	•							
Berlaimont			•					
Bouchain			•					Evening
Bourbourg		•						
Cambrai			•		•			
Cassel			•					
Condé sur l'Escaut					•			
Coudekerque Branche		•						
Cysoing		•						
Denain			•					
Douai		•		•	•			
Dunkerque		•			•			
Fourmies					•			
Grande Synthe		•	•					
Gravlines; pl Charles Valentin					•			
Hautmont		•			•			
Hazebrouck: pl du G. de Gaulle	•							
Hondschoote					•			
La Bassée			•					
Landrecies					•			
Le Quesnoy					•			
Lille: Concorde: av Verhaeren					•			
Lille: D' Hellemmes: pl Hentges		•			•			
Lille: de Fives: pl Madeleine Caulier		•	•					
Lille: de La Vieille Bourse: pl de G.Gaulle		•	•	•	•	•	•	

Location	M	T	W	Th	F	S	Su	Comments
Lille: Deliot: pl Deliot						•		
Lille: Edith Cavll: rue de F.des Postes					•			
Lille: Pellevoisin: Devant l'Église			•					
Lille: pl du Concert			•		•			
Lille: pl du Général de Gaulle							•	2nd & 4th Sunday Organic produce
Lille: pl Nouvelle avnture		•	•	•	•	•	•	
Lille: pl Sébastopol			•		•			
Lille: St-Sauveur: av Kennedy		•						
Lille: Vauban: pl Catinat					•			Afternoon from 15.00 to 19.00
Lille: Wazemmes: pl de la Nouvelle avnture		•		•			•	
Marchiennes					•			
Marcoing		•						
Marcq en Baroeul						•		Saturday evening
Maubeuge: pl de l'Industrie	•					•		
Merville			•					
Orchies					•		•	
Roubaix: rue Rubens	•	•	•	•	•	•	•	Friday & Saturday afternoon
Seclin: centre ville	•							
Solesmes			•					
Solre le Château		•						
St-Amand les Eaux: pl de Sentament					•			
Steenvoorde					•			
Tourcoing: pl de la Résistance	•		•					
Trélon	•							
Valenciennnes			•			•		
Villeneuve d'Ascq		•	•			•		Saturday evening
Wormhout			•					

Department of Pas de Calais

Location	M	T	W	Th	F	S	Su	Comments
Aire sur la Lys: pl Notre Dame					•			
Ardres			•					
Arques: pl Roger Salengro		•						
Arras: pl de la Vacquerie			•			•		
Arras: pl des Héros			•			•		
Arras: pl Marc Lanvin				•				
Arras: pl Verlaine							•	
Auchel: pls J.Guesde & A.Marcey		•			•			
Audruicq: pl du G. de Gaulle			•					
Auxi le Château: pl de la Mairie						•		
Avion: pl J.Duclos				•				
Bapaume: pl Faidherbe					•			
Barlin: pl Salengro			•					
Berck Plage: pl de l'Eglise			•		•			
Berck Ville: pl de la Mairie		•			•		•	
Béthune: Grand place	•							
Béthune: pl Lamartine	•							
Boulogne: pl Dalton			•			•		
Boulogne: pl Damrémont							•	
Boulogne: pl Vignon							•	

Location	M	T	W	Th	F	S	Su	Comments
Bruay en Artois							•	
Bully les Mines			•		•			
Calais: pl d' Armes			•		•			
Calais: ZUP du Beau Marais							•	
Camiers: pl Communale	•							
Condette							•	Afternoon June to September
Courrières			•					
Desvres		•					•	Sunday at Fauborg d'Isle
Equihen Plage: pl Albert Bécart			•					Afternoon
Étaples: pl de la Mairie		•			•			
Fauquembergues: Grand place				•				
Fiennes		•						
Frévent: pl du Marché		•						
Fruges: pl du Général de Gaulle						•		
Guînes: pl Foch					•			
Harnes				•				
Hesdin: main square				•				
Houdain				•				
Hucqueliers			•					
Le Portel: pl de l' Église		•			•			
Le Touquet: pl rue de Metz	•			•		•		Monday & Saturday June - September
Lens		•			•			
Licques: centre ville	•							
Liéven			•					
Lillers					•			
Lumbres			•					
Marquise		•	•					Wednesday at Place de l'Hotel de Ville
Montreuil:Grand place					•			
Noeux les Mines				•				
Outreau: pl de la Mairie	•			•				
Samer: Grand pl Foch	•							
Sangatte: pl de la Mairie					•			
St-Martin: pl Aristide Briand				•				
St-Omer: pl Foch					•			
St-Pol sur Ternoise: centre ville	•							
Vimy					•			
Wimeraux: pl de la Mairie		•			•			
Wissant: rue Gambetta			•					

Can you cross The Channel in a different style?

Yes you Can Can.

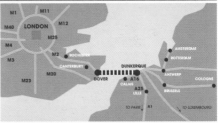

DEPARTMENTS

Calvados	(14)
Eure	(27)
Manche	(50)
Orne	(61)
Seine Maritime	(76)

Department of Calvados

Location	M	T	W	Th	F	S	Su	Comments
Argences: pl de la République				•				
Arromanches		•			•			
Asnelles: pl Alexandeur Stamier				•				seasonal
Aunay sur Odon: rue du 12 Juin					•			
Balleroy		•						
Bayeux			•		•			
Beaumont en Auge					•			
Bernières sur Mer				•				
Blainville sur Orne					•			
Blangy le Château				•				
Blonville sur Mer: centre ville		•			•			July & August
Bonnebosq			•					
Bretteville sur Laize	•			•				
Cabourg	•		•				•	Daily in season
Caen: boulevard Leroy			•		•			
Caen: Chemin Vert				•				
Caen: Grâce de Dieu		•						
Caen: Guérinierè				•				
Caen: Pierre-Heuzé				•	•			
Caen: pl. St.Sauveur					•			
Caen: rue de Bayeux		•						
Caen: St-Pierre							•	
Caen: Venoix			•					
Cahagnes					•			
Cairon			•				•	
Calvaire St-Pierre			•					
Cambremer					•		•	Traditional & ancient markets July & August
Carpiquet							•	
Caumont l' Éventé				•				
Clécy							•	
Condé sur Noireau				•				

Location	M	T	W	Th	F	S	Su	Comments
Courseulles sur Mer: Police Municipale		•			•			
Creully			•					
Deauville		•			•			Daily in season
Démouville		•				•		
Dives sur Mer		•				•		Tuesday seasonal
Douvres la Délivrande				•	•			
Dozulé		•						
Évrecy			•					
Falaise					•			
Fervaques							•	seasonal
Fleury sur Orne					•			
Fontenay le Marmion				•				
Giberville			•					
Grandcamp Maisy		•				•	•	Saturday & Sunday seasonal
Graye sur Mer				•				
Hermanville sur Mer		•						
Hérouville St-Clair		•	•		•			
Honfleur			•		•			
Houlgate				•				Daily in season
Ifs		•						
Isigny sur Mer		•			•			
La Rivière St-Sauveur				•			•	Sunday farm produce July to September
Landelles et Coupigny			•					
Langrune sur Mer	•				•			Monday seasonal
Le Bény Bocage				•				
Le Molay Littry		•		•		•		
Lion sur Mer				•				
Lisieux			•		•		•	Friday cattle market & local produce
Wednesday afternoons								
Livarot				•				
Louvigny					•			
Luc sur Mer			•		•			Wednesday seasonal
May sur Orne				•				
Merville Franceville				•				seasonal
Mézidon Canon			•			•		
Mondeville: qrt Charlotte Cordet		•	•					
Mouen					•			
Moyaux						•		
Noyers Bocage						•		
Orbec		•						Farm produce July to September
Ouistreham: Riva Bella		•			•	•		Saturday seasonal
Pont d' Ouilly						•		
Pont l' Évêque	•							Small market in winter
Port en Bessin Huppain						•		
Potigny			•					
Soliers				•				
St-Aubin sur Mer				•				
St-Julien le Faucon							•	seasonal
St-Martin des Besaces				•				
St-Pierre sur Dives	•							
St-Sever					•			

Location	M	T	W	Th	F	S	Su	Comments
Thaon			•					
Thury Harcourt		•						
Tilly sur Seulles							•	
Touques		•			•			
Trévières				•				
Troarn					•			
Trouville sur Mer				•			•	Daily in season
Varaville				•			•	
Vassy		•						
Verson					•			
Vierville sur Mer	•							
Villers Bocage				•				
Villers sur Mer: pl de la Mairie		•			•			Daily in season
Villerville		•			•			
Vire					•			

Department of Eure

Location	M	T	W	Th	F	S	Su	Comments
Aubevoye							•	
Beaumesnil	•							
Beaumont le Roger: pl de l'Eglise		•		•				
Bernay					•			
Beuzeville: pl du marché		•						
Boissey le Chatel				•				
Bourg Achard: pl de la Mairie	•							
Bourgtheroulde					•			
Breteuil sur Iton			•					
Brionne				•			•	
Broglie				•				
Carsix							•	Afternoon
Charleval					•			
Conches en Ouche				•			•	
Cormeilles				•				
Damville		•						
Épaignes							•	
Étrépagny			•					Wednesday afternoon clothing only
Évreux: Centre			•		•			
Évreux: la Madelaine					•		•	Friday afternoon
Évreux: Navarre							•	
Évreux: Nétreville				•				
Évreux: St-Michel		•		•				
Ézy sur Eure				•			•	
Fleury sur Andelle		•			•			
Gaillon: rue du G. de Gaulle		•						
Gasny					•			
Gisors	•							
Giverville							•	
Harcourt					•			
Ivry la Bataille					•			
La Barre en Ouche			•					

Location	M	T	W	Th	F	S	Su	Comments
La Bonneville sur Iton					•			
La Croix St-Leufroy		•						
La Ferrière sur Risle							•	
La Neuve Lyre	•							
Le Fidelaire							•	
Le Neubourg	•		•					Monday Livestock
Le Vaudreuil							•	
Léry		c						
Les Andelys						•		Saturday all day
Lieurey			•		•			
Louviers			•		•			Saturday all day
Lyons la Forêt			•		•	•		
Ménilles							•	
Montfort sur Risle		•						
Montreuil l'Argillé: pl de la Mairie		•						
Nonancourt			•					
Pacy sur Eure				•				
Pas de marchés		•						Afternoon
Perriers sur Andrelle					•			
Pont Audemer: rue de la République	•				•			Monday & Friday all day
Pont de l'Arche							•	
Pont St-Pierre					•			
Quillebeuf sur Seine			•					All day
Romilly sur Andelle			•					All day
Routot			•					
Rugles					•			
St-André de l'Eure				•				
St-Georges du Vièvre			•					
St-Pierre du Vauvray							•	
Thiberville: rue de la République	•							
Tillièrres sur Avre							•	
Val de Reuil					•			Afternoon
Verneuil sur Avre						•		
Vernon			•			•		Saturday all day

Department of Manche

Location	M	T	W	Th	F	S	Su	Comments
Agneaux	•							
Avranches: d'Estouteville		•				•		Tuesday seasonal
Barfleur		•				•		Tuesday seasonal
Barneville Carteret				•		•	•	Thursday & Sunday seasonal
Beaumont Hague						•		
Brécey				•				
Bréhal		•						
Bricquebec: pl St-Anne	•							
Canisy				•				
Carentan: centre ville	•							
Carolles			•					
Cérences			•				•	Sunday seasonal
Cerisy la Forêt			•					

Location	M	T	W	Th	F	S	Su	Comments
Cerisy la Salle						•		
Cherbourg		•		•		•		
Cherbourg: les Halles	•	•	•	•	•	•	•	
Condé sur Vire			•					
Coulouvray Boisbenâtre						•		
Coutainville le Passous		•				•		
Coutances				•				
Créances							•	
Ducey		•						
Équeurdreville		•			•			
Flamanville			•					
Gavray						•		Livestock 1st & 3rd Thursday evenings
Genets							•	seasonal
Gouville: pl de la Mairie	•				•			Monday seasonal
Granville: cours Jonville			•		•			
Hambye		•						
Hauteville sur Mer		•	•	•	•	•	•	Daily in season except Monday
Jullouville		•			•			Tuesday seasonal
Juvigny le Tertre	•			•				
Kairon							•	seasonal
La Haye du Puits			•					
La Haye Pesnel			•					
Le Teilleul				•				
Les Pieux					•			
Lessay		•						
Marigny			•					
Montebourg					•			
Montmartin sur Mer			•					
Mortain					•			
Notre Dame de Cenilly		•						
Octeville			•				•	
Percy					•			
Périers					•			
Picauville				•				
Piron			•		•		•	Wednesday & Friday seasonal
Pontorson			•					
Portbail		•						
Quettehou		•						
Quettrville sur Sienne						•		
Roncey					•			
Sartilly					•			
Sourdeval		•						
St-Clair sur Elle		•						
St-Hilaire du Harcoët			•		•			
St-James: centre ville	•							
St-Jean de Daye					•			
St-Jean le Thomas							•	seasonal
St-Lô			•		•	•		
St-Martin de Bréhal							•	seasonal
St-Mère-Église			•					
St-Pair			•					

Location	M	T	W	Th	F	S	Su	Comments
St-Pierre Église			•					
St-Pois				•				
St-Sauveur le Vicomte					•			
St-Sauveur Lendelin				•				
St-Vaast la Hougue					•			
Tessy sur Vire				•				
Torigni sur Virepl du Château	•							
Valognes					•			
Villedieu les Poêles		•						

Department of Orne

Location	M	T	W	Th	F	S	Su	Comments
Alençon: centre ville				•		•	•	
Argentan: pl St-Germain		•			•		•	
Athis de l'Orne: Mairie		•						
Bagnoles de L'Orne		•			•			
Bellême				•				
Bretoncelles				•	•			
Briouze: pl G. de Gaulle	•							
Carrouges			•					
Ceauce				•				
Ceton							•	
Condé sur Huisne					•			
Courtomer					•		•	
Crulai							•	
Damigny			•					
Domfront					•			
Écouché					•			
Flers		•			•			
Gacé					•			
L' Aigle		•			•			
La Chapelle d'Andaine					•			
La Conception		•						
La Ferté Frêsnel				•				
La Ferté Macé				•				
Le Mele sur Sarthe			•					
Le Merlerault				•				
Le Sap		•			•			
Le Theil sur Huisne			•					
Longny au Perche			•					
Messei				•				
Montilly sur Noireau							•	
Mortagne au Perche					•			
Mortrée							•	
Moulins la Marche				•				
Nocé		•						
Passais		•						
Pervenchères		•						
Putanges Pont Écrepin				•				
Ranes					•			

Location	M	T	W	Th	F	S	Su	Comments
Rémalard: pl G. de Gaulle	•							
Sées						•		
Soligny la Trappe		•						Livestock
St-Colombe			•		•			
St-Gauburge			•		•			
Tesse la Madeleine			•	•				
Tinchebray	•							
Tourouvre					•			
Trun				•				
Vimoutiers: pl du Pays d'Auge	•							

Department of Seine Maritime

Location	M	T	W	Th	F	S	Su	Comments
Auffay: centre					•			
Aumale: pl du Marché					•			
Bacqueville en Caux: pl du G. de Gaulle			•				•	
Barentin: pl du Commandant Dubosc					•			
Bellencombre		•						
Bihorel			•		•			
Blangy sur Bresle							•	
Bois Guillaume			•	•				
Bolbec: pl Chales de Gaulle	•							
Bonsecours				•				
Bosc le Hard			•					
Buchy: centre ville	•							
Cantelau			•		•			
Cany Barville: pl Robert Gabel	•							
Caudebec en Caux					•			
Caudebec lès Elbeuf							•	
Clères					•			Friday afternoon
Criel sur Mer			•				•	Sunday seasonal
Criquetot l'Esneval				•				
Darnétal			•				•	Wednesday afternoon
Deville les Rouen							•	
Dieppe					•			
Doudeville					•			
Duclair		•						
Elbeuf					•			
Envermeu					•			
Étretat				•				
Eu					•			
Fauville en Caux					•			
Fécamp					•			All day
Fontaine le Dun			•					
Forges les Eaux			•				•	
Foucarmont		•						
Goderville		•						
Gonfreville l'Orcher				•				
Gonneville la Mallet			•					
Gournay en Bray		•		•				

Location	M	T	W	Th	F	S	Su	Comments
Grand Quevilly		•	•	•	•	•		
Harfleur							•	
La Bouille			•					
La Feuillie				•				
Le Havre				•				
Le Trait					•			
Le Tréport		•			•			
Les Grandes Ventes			•					Wednesday afternoon
Lillebonne			•					
Londinières				•				Thursday afternoon
Longueville sur scie							•	
Luneray							•	
Maromme			•			•		Saturday afternoon
Mont St-Aignan			•					
Montivilliers				•				
Montville					•			
Neufchâtel en Bray					•			
Offranville				•				
Pavilly			•					
Petit Couronne				•				
Petit Quevilly							•	
Rouen: Aucun	•							
Rouen: Ile Lacroix			•					
Rouen: La Grand Mare					•			
Rouen: pl de la Calende		•		•				General markets open all day
Rouen: pl des Emmurées		•	•			•		All day
Rouen: pl du Boulingrin			•					
Rouen: pl du Vieux Marché		•	•	•	•	•	•	Food & flower markets, mornings
Rouen: pl St-Marc		•			•	•		All day
Rouen: rue Cauchoise				•				Local & speciality produce.
Rouen: rue Grieu		•						
Rouen: Sapins Châtelet			•					
Rouen: St-Clément			•					
Ry					•			
Sotteville les Rouen			•		•			
St-Etienne du Rouvray			•			•		
St-Nicolas d'Aliermont						•		
St-Romain de Colbosq					•			
St-Saëns			•					
St-Valery en Caux				•			•	Sunday seasonal
Tôtes			•					
Veules les Roses			•					
Yerville		•						
Yport			•					
Yvetot			•					

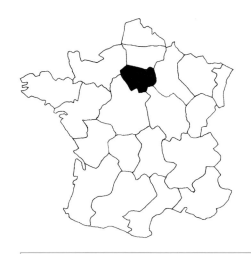

DEPARTMENTS

Paris	(75)
Seine et Marne	(77)
Yvelines	(78)
Essone	(91)
Hauts de Seine	(92)
Seine St Denis	(93)
Val de Marne	(94)
Val d'Oise	(95)

Department of Paris

Location	arr	M	T	W	Th	F	S	Su	Comments
Enfants Rouge	03	•	•	•	•	•	•	•	rue de Bretagne
Temple	03		•	•	•	•	•	•	rues Eugène-Spuller & Dupetit-Thouars 9:00 - 19:00
Loius Lépine	04	•	•	•	•	•	•		pl Louis Lépine & quays 8:00 - 19:30
Maubert	05		•		•		•		pl Maubert 8:00 - 13:30
Monge	05			•		•		•	pl Monge 8:00 - 13:30
Port Royal	05		•		•		•		bd de Port Royal
Raspail	06				•		•	•	rues du Cherch Midi & Rennes Sunday organic food
St-Germain	06		•	•	•	•	•	•	4/8 rue Lobineau 8:00 - 13:30
Saxe Breteuil	07				•		•		av de Saxe
Batignolles	08						•		bd des Batignolles 8:00 - 13:30
Europe	08	•	•	•	•	•	•		1 rue Corvetto
Madeleine	08	•	•	•	•	•	•		pl de la Madelaine 8:00 - 19:30
Postmark: Champs Elysées	08			•		•	•		avs Marigny & Gabriel all day
Alibert	10							•	rue Albert
St-Martin	10	•	•	•	•	•	•		rue Château d' Eau
St-Quentin	10	•	•	•	•	•	•	•	85 bis bd de Magenta
Bastille	11				•			•	bd Richard Lenoir
Belleville	11		•			•			bd de Belleville
Charonne	11			•			•		rues Charonne & Alex Dumas
Père Lachaise	11		•			•			bd de Ménilmontan
Popincourt	11		•			•			rues Oberkampf & Crussol
Cours de Vincennes	12			•			•		bd Picpus & & rue Arnold Netter
Daumesnil	12		•			•			bd de Reuilly & rue Charenton & pl FelixEboué
Ledru Rollin	12				•		•		av Ledru Rollin
Pl d'Aligre	12	•	•	•	•	•	•	•	Charenton & Crozatier 7:30 - 13:00
Poniatowski	12				•			•	av Daumesnil & rue Picpus
St-Eloi	12				•			•	rue de Reuilly
Auguste Blanqui	13		•			•		•	pl Italie & rue Barrault
Bobillot	13		•			•		•	pl Rungis & rue de la Colonie
Jeanne d'Arc	13				•			•	pl Jeanne d' Arc
Maison Blanche	13				•			•	110-162 av d' Italie

Location	arr	M	T	W	Th	F	S	Su	Comments
Salpêtrière	13	•			•				bd de l' Hôpital
Vincent Auriol	13		•			•			bd Vincent Auriol
Brune	14			•				•	impasse Vandal & bd Brune
Edgar Quinet	14		•			•			centre bd E.Quinet
Mouton	14	•			•			•	rues Brézin,Saillard,Mouton,Duvernet & Boulard all day
Villemain	14		•					•	av Villemain & rue d' Alesia
Cervantes	15		•			•			rues Bargue & de la Procession
Conventioner	15	•		•				•	rues Al Chartier & Abbé Groult
Grenelle	15		•					•	rues Lourmel & du Commerce
Lecourbe	15		•			•			rues Vasco da Gama & Leblanc
Lefebvre	15		•			•			rues Olivier de Serres & Dantzig
St-Charles	15	•			•				rue Javel & rond point St-Charles
Amiral Bruix	16		•			•			rues Weber & Marbeau
Auteuil	16		•			•			rues Donizette & la Fontaine
Gros la Fontaine	16	•			•				rues Gros & la Fontaine
Passy	16	•	•	•	•	•	•	•	8:00 - 19:30 Sunday morning
Point du Jour	16	•		•				•	av de Versailles & rues Marois & Gudin
Porte Molitor	16	•			•				pl de la Porte Molitor
President Wilsonse	16		•			•			rue Debrousse & Pl d' Iéna
St-Didier	16	•	•	•	•	•	•	•	rues Mesnil & St-Didier market all day. Sunday morning
Batignolles	17	•	•	•	•	•	•	•	96 bis rue Lemercier all day. Sunday morning
BerthieReims	17		•			•			bd de Reims & sq Aulmann
Navier	17	•			•				rues Lantiez & Epinettes
Ternes	17	•	•	•	•	•	•	•	8 bis rue Lebon 8:00 - 19:30
Barbès	18		•			•			bd Chapelle, hospital Lariboisière
La Chapelle	18							•	10 rue l' Olive all day. Sunday morning
Ney	18		•					•	rues Jean Varenne & Camille Flammarion
Ordener	18		•			•			rues Montcalm & Championet
Ornano	18			•				•	rues Mt-Cenis & Ordener
Jean Jaurès	19	•		•					rues Ourq & Ardennes
Joinville	19			•				•	rues Joinville & Jomard
Place des Fêtes	19	•			•				pl des Fetes
Porte Brunet	19		•			•			av de la P.Brunet
Riquet	19	•	•	•	•	•	•	•	rue Riquet all day. Sunday morning
Secrétan	19	•	•	•	•	•	•	•	33 av de Secrétan all day. Sunday morning
Villette	19		•			•			27 & 41 bd de la Villette
Belgrand	20		•			•			rues Belgr&e & Chine & pl Piaf
Davout	20	•		•					av de la Porte de Montreuil & rue Mendelsson
Mortier	20			•				•	av de la Porte de Ménilmontant & Maurice Berteaux
Pyrénées	20			•				•	rues de l' Ermitage & de Ménilmontant
Réunion	20			•				•	pl de la Réunion
Télégraphe	20		•			•			rue de Télégraphe & Belleville cemetary

Department of Seine et Marne

Location	M	T	W	Th	F	S	Su	Comments
Avon: La Butte Montceau				•				
Beton Bazoches: pl de l' Église	•							
Bois le Roi: Parking de la Gare				•			•	
Boitron: pl du Monument aux morts							•	2nd Sunday
Bray sur Seine: centre ville					•			

Location	M	T	W	Th	F	S	Su	Comments
Brie Comte Robert: pl du Marché			•		•	•		
Brou sur Chantereine: av de la République		•			•			
Bussy St-Georges: pl de Verdun					•			
Champagne sur Seine: pl Roland Dorgeles				•	•			
Champs sur Marne: pl du Bois de Grâce					•			
Château Landon: pl du Marché				•				
Chaumes en Brie: pl Foch		•						
Chelles: parc de Souvenir		•		•			•	
Chevry Cossigny: pl de la Mairie			•					
Claye Souilly: pl Général de Gaulle			•		•			
Cocherel							•	Country market on the 3rd Sunday.
Collegien: pl de la Mairie					•			
Combs la Ville: route de Varennes			•		•			
Coulommiers: centre ville			•				•	
Coulommiers: Ville haute					•			
Courtry: Route de Chat					•			
Crécy la Chapelle: centre ville			•					
Crovy sur Ourcq: pl du Marché							•	2nd Sunday
Dammarie les Lys: pl du marché						•		Saturday afternoon
Dammartin en Goële: pl de l' Église			•					
Donnemarie Dontilly: pl du Marché	•							
Echouboulains: centre ville				•				
Égreville: Halle couverte	•							
Esbly: pl de l' Europe			•					
Faremoutiers: pl Général de Gaulle				•				
Fericy: rue de Ferland			•					
Fontainebleau: pl de la République		•		•			•	
Fontenay Trésigny: pl de l'Ancienne Gare							•	
Gretz Armainvilliers: rue Thiers		•		•				
Guérard: pl de la Mairie			•					
Guignes: Face à l' Église			•					
Jouarre							•	2nd Sunday
Jouy le Châtel: pl du 19 Mars 1962		•						
La Chapelle la Reine: pl de la République		•						
La Ferté Gaucher: pl du Général de Gaulle				•			•	
La Fertè sous Jouarre: bd de Turennes		•		•				
La Rochette: pl Arnand de la Rochette		•		•				
Lagny sur Marne: pl du Marché au Blé			•	•			•	
Le Châtelet en Brie: pl de l' Église		•				•		Saturday all day
Le Mée sur Seine: Allée de la Gare						•		Afternoon
Lesigny: centre comm. du Parc			•					
Lésigny: centre ville					•			
Lieusaint: pl du Colombier					•			
Lizy sur Ourcq: pl du Marché				•				
Lizy sur Ourcq: rues Curie et Gallieni							•	Country market
Longueville: pl de la Mairie				•				
Lorrez le Bocage: pl de la Mairie		•					•	
Meaux: bd Jean ROSE Place		•						
Meaux: Guymner: Pierre COLINET				•				
Meaux: pl de Beauval							•	
Meaux: quart. du Marché Centre					•			Until 14.00pm

Location	M	T	W	Th	F	S	Su	Comments
Melun: Mail Gaillardon			•		•			
Melun: rue de l' Industrie							•	
Melun: rue Emile LECLERC				•				
Mitry Mory: pl Salvatore ALLENDE		•			•			
Moissy Cramayel: pl du 14 Juillet		•		•				
Montereau Fault Yonne: Surville				•				Afternoon
Montereau Fault Yonne: Surville							•	
Montereau Fault Yonne: Ville basse			•		•			
Montéurain: Rue Maucegard					•			
Montry: pl de la Mairie		•			•			
Moret sur Loing: centre ville		•		•				
Mormant: rue Général Leclerc				•				
Mortcerf: pl de la Mairie				•				
Nangis: Halle et centre ville			•		•			
Nemours: pl du Champs de Mars			•		•			
Noisiel: Cours des Roches			•		•		•	16.00 to 19.30
Noisiel: pl Emile MEUNIER				•				
Othis: pl de la Mairie					•			
Ozoir la Ferrière: pl des Sports			•		•			
Ozouer leVoulgis: pl de l' Église				•			•	
Pontault Combault: marché couvert Gare				•				
Pontault Combault: pl de l' Église					•			Afternoon organic produce
Pontault Combault: pl Louis ARAGON		•			•			
Provins: pl H. Balzac						•		
Rebais: pl du Marché		•						
Roissy en Brie: Rue Pasteur					•			
Rozay en Brie: rue Général de Gaulle					•			
Saâcy sur Marne: pl de la Mairie					•			
Samois sur Seine: pl de la Mairie					•			
Savigny le Temple: Ctre Com du Miroir d' Eau			•		•			
Souppes sur Loing: pl de l' Église							•	
St-Fargeau Ponthierry: pl Jacques MADELIN				•			•	
St-Germain sur Morin: pl de la Gare			•				•	
St-Mammès: quai de Seine							•	
St-Mard: pl de la Libération			•		•			
St-Pathus: pl du Centre Commercial			•					
St-Soupplets: pl de l' Église				•				
Thomery: pl de l' Église		•						
Torcy: L' Arche GUEDON			•		•		•	
Torcy: pl de l' Église					•			
Tournan en Brie: pl du Marché			•		•			
Trilport: pl du 19 Mars 1962				•				
Vaires sur Marne: rue de Chelles			•				•	
Varennes sur Seine: pl de l' Église				•				
Veneux les Sablons: av de Fontainebleau					•			
Vernou la Celle sur Seine: pl de l' Église			•					
Vert St-Denis: Terrain du Cheval			•	•				
Villeparisis: pl du Marché			•	•				
Villiers St-Georges: pl de la Mairie							•	
Villiers sur Morin: pl de l' Église					•			
Voulx: rue Durocher			•					

Department of Yvelines								
Location	M	T	W	Th	F	S	Su	Comments
Ablis: pl de l'Église					•			
Andresy: bd Noel Marc						•		
Andresy: Promenade Docteur Giffard			•					
Aubergenville		•				•		
Bailly: pl du Marché			•			•		
Beynes: pl du 8 mai 1945					•		•	
Bois d'Arcy			•			•		
Bonnières sur Seine: pl de la Libération							•	
Bouafle: pl de la Mairie					•			
Bougival: centre Bouzemont			•		•			
Breval: pl du Mal Leclerc					•			
Buc: pl du marché					•			
Buchelay: rue P.Curie							•	
Carrieres sous Poissy: St-Louis					•			
Carrieres sur Seine: bvd Carnot		•			•		•	
Châteaufort: pl St-Christophet			•		•			Afternoons
Chatou: av de Montparnasse				•			•	
Chatou: pl Maurice Bertaux			•		•			
Chatou: sq Debussy		•			•			
Chavnay: centre Cial de Chavnay					•			
Conflans Ste-Honorine: pl Fouillière		•			•		•	
Conflans Ste-Honorine: pl Romagné			•		•			
Conflans Ste-Honorine: Rés du Maréchaux				•			•	
Croissy sur Seine: bvd Hostachy				•	•			
Feucherolles: pl de la Poste				•				
Flins Sur Seine: pl de Château							•	
Fontenay le Fleury: av Jean Lurcat		•			•		•	
Fourqueux: pl Victor Hugo			•					
Guyancourt: pl du Marché			•		•			
Houdan: pl de l' Église					•			
Houilles: pl de la Victoire				•			•	
Houilles: rue Gambetta-av Carnot			•		•			
L' Etang La Ville: pl du marché			•		•			
La Celle St-Cloud: av A.R.Gilbert		•			•			
La Celle St-Cloud: pl Berthet			•		•			
La Celle St-Cloud: pl Mal Leclerc				•			•	
La Celle St-Cloud: village							•	
La Queue les Yvelines: pl du Mon.aux Morts						•		
Le Chesnay: rue des Deux Frères		•			•			
Le Mesnil le Roi: rue du Haute de la Girouette				•				
Le Mesnil le Roi: rue E Fontanier				•				
Le Perray en Yvelines: av de la Gare		•						
Le Perray en Yvelines: rue de Paris					•			
Le Port Marly: rue de Paris					•			
Le Vesinet: marché du centre		•			•			
Le Vesinet: pl des Charmettes			•		•			
Le Vesinet: pl du Marché		•			•			
Le Vésinet: qrt Princesse			•		•			
Le Vesinet: rond point de la République				•			•	

Location	M	T	W	Th	F	S	Su	Comments
Les Clayes Sous Bois: centre ville				•			•	
Les Essarts Le Roi: pl du 8 Mai 1945		•		•				
Les Mureaux: pl de la République					•			
Limay: pl du Marché		•		•				
Louveciennes: pl des combattants			•		•			
Magny les Hameaux: pl du 19 mars 1962					•			Afternoon
Magny les Hameaux: rue lemarchand	•	•		•				
Maisons Laffitte: pl de Marché			•		•			
Mantes la Jolie: centre comm. Mantes 2		•			•			Friday afternoon
Mantes la Jolie: centre ville			•		•			
Mantes la Ville: pl du Marché				•	•			
Maule: pl du G.Gaulle					•			
Maurepas: pl du Marché			•		•			
Meulan: pl de l'Aubette	•				•			
Meulan: qrt du Paradis							•	
Meulan: Rue de la Ferme							•	
Montainville: pl de la Mairie					•			
Montesson: rue du Gal Leclerc			•				•	
Montfort l`Amaury: pl du Palais			•					
Montigny le Bretonneux: pl E.Marcel					•			
Montigny le Bretonneux: pl E.Marcel-sud canal			•		•			
Montigny le Bretonneux: pl J.Couer(Sourderie)		•		•				
Montigny le Bretonneux: pl Jacques Couer							•	
Neauphle le Châteaux: pl de marché	•	•						Fair 5th December
Orgerus: pl des Halles		•						
Orgeval: pl de l' Église					•			
Plaisir: Halle du Marché		•			•		•	
Poissy: Beauregard			•		•			
Poissy: pl de la République		•			•		•	
Porcheville: pl Adam			•					
Rambouillet: La Clairière					•			
Rambouillet: La Louvière							•	
Rambouillet: pl Felix Faure					•			
Rambouillet: pl Marie Roux		•			•			
Rosny sur Seine: pl du marché			•					
Sartrouville: marché de la gare					•			Afternoon
Sartrouville: rue de Tocqueville		•			•			
Sartrouville: rue Lamartine			•				•	
Septeuil: pl de la Mairie			•					
St-Arnoult en Yvelines: rue Henri Grivot							•	
St-Cyr L'École: rue Marceau-rue Gard		•			•			
St-Germain en Laye: C.C.Coteaux Bel Air			•		•			Saturday all day
St-Germain en Laye: pl Ch.Frahier			•		•			
St-Germain en Laye: pl du marché neuf		•		•			•	
St-Leger en Yvelines: pl du Gros Billot					•			Afternoon
St-Nom le Breteche: halles couvert		•		•				
St-Remy les Chevreuses: rue Ditte			•		•			
Trappes: pl de la Mairie-pl Merisiers		•		•	•			
Triel sur Seine: Espace Senet			•					
Vaux sur Seine: rue Louvet					•			
Vélizy Villacoublay: le Mail		•			•			

Location	M	T	W	Th	F	S	Su	Comments
Velizy Villacoublay: Mozart		•			•		•	
Verneuil sur Seine: pl du marché			•					
Vernouillet: pl du G.Gaulle					•			
Versailles: av de St-Cloud		•			•		•	
Versailles: Carré à l' Avoine				•				
Versailles: pl du marché Notre-Dame		•	•		•	•		
Versailles: rue Bonne avnture					•			
Versailles: rue de la Cathédrale					•			
Versailles: Square Lamome			•		•			
Villennes sur Seine: pl de l' Église				•	•			
Villepreux: av des Clayes			•		•			
Viroflay: av du Gen. Leclerc	•		•		•			
Viroflay: pl de Verdun			•		•		•	

Department of Essone

Location	M	T	W	Th	F	S	Su	Comments
Angerville: pl Tessier		•						
Arpajon: pl du Marché					•			
Athis Mons: Gravilliers				•			•	
Athis Mons: pl de la Gare					•			Organic produce
Ballancourt sur Essonne: rue de l' Aunette				•			•	
Bièvres: pl de la Mairie			•			•		Saturday afternoon
Boissy sous St-Yon: pl de la Mairie		•	•					
Bondoufle: centre ville			•		•			
Bouray sur Juine: pl de l' Église		•			•			
Boussy St-Antoine: centre ville				•	•	•	•	
Brétigny sur Orge: pl du Marché				•		•		
Breuillet: pl de l' Église				•		•		
Brunoy: Bosserons		•			•			
Brunoy: Centre				•		•		
Brunoy: Mardelles			•					
Bruyeres le Chatel: pl Simon					•			
Bures sur Yvette: rue ChArles de Gaulle			•		•			
Chilly Mazarin: pl de la Libération		•		•			•	
Corbeil Essonnes: Montconseil			•		•			
Corbeil Essonnes: Moulin Galant			•		•			
Corbeil Essonnes: pl Salengro		•			•		•	
Corbeil Essonnes: pl Thorez				•			•	
Corbeil Essonnes: Tarterêts					•			
Courcouronnes: centre comm. Thorigny							•	
Crosne: av Jean Jaurès					•		•	
Dourdan: pl de l' Église			•		•			
Dravil: pl de la République				•	•			
Dravil: Rond Point des Fêtes		•			•			
Épinay sous Sénart: centre comm.			•			•	•	
Épinay sur Orge: rue Guy Moquet					•			
Estouches: pl de l' Hôtel de Ville					•			
Étampes: pl St-Gilles		•						
Étréchy: pl ChArles de Gaulle							•	
Évry: Lieutenant Buisson		•			•			

Location	M	T	W	Th	F	S	Su	Comments
Évry: pl Jules Vallès			•				•	Wednesday afternoon
Évry: rue de Château			•		•			
Gif sur Yvette: Marché du Parc				•			•	
Gif sur Yvette: quart. De Chevry			•		•			
Grigny				•			•	
Igny: Gommonvilliers				•			•	
Igny: pl Mendès France			•		•			
Itteville: centre ville				•	•			
Juvisy sur Orge: pl du Maréchal Leclerc			•		•			
La Ferté Alais: pl du Marché			•		•			
Les Ulis: centre comm. Chapms Lasniers:		•			•		•	
Limours en Hurepoix: pl de la Mairie				•			•	
Linas: pl de la Mairie			•		•			
Lisses: Mail de l'Ile de France		•		•				Thursday afternoon
Longjumeau: pl Bretten			•		•			
Maisse: pl de l' Église			•					
Marcoussis: pl de la République				•	•	•	•	
Marolles en Hurepoix: pl de la Mairie					•			
Massy: centre ville				•	•	•	•	
Massy: qrt Narbonne et Graviers		•	•		•			
Massy: quart. Villaine			•		•			
Mennecy: pl de la Mairie			•		•			
Méréville: Hôtel de Ville				•				
Milly la Forêt: pl des halles			•					Afternoon
Montgeron: pl Joffre			•				•	
Montgeron: St-Hubert		•			•			
Montlhéry: pl du Marché	•		•					
Morsang sur Orge: pl du Marché			•		•			
Orsay: centre		•	•	•	•		•	Organic produce on Sunday
Orsay: Mondétour			•	•	•		•	
Palaiseau: centre ville			•	•	•		•	
Palaiseau: Le Pileu			•		•			
Palaiseau: Lozère			•					
Pussay: pl du Carouge	•							
Quincy sous Sénart: rue de Boissy St-Léger			•				•	
Ris Orangis: Le Plateau		•	•	•	•			
Ris Orangis: rue Edmond Bonté			•	•	•		•	
Saclay: Le Val d' Albian		•			•			
Savigny sur Orge: pl Davout		•			•		•	
Savigny sur Orge: pl Jules Ferry			•		•			Saturday afternoon
St-Chéron: pl de la gare					•			
St-Chéron: pl de la poste			•					
St-Michel sur Orge: marché Gambetta			•		•			
Ste-Geneviève des Bois			•	•			•	Friday afternoon
Verrieres le Buisson: pl Charles de Gaulle			•		•			
Vigneux sur Seine: av Henri Barbusse			•	•			•	
Vigneux sur Seine: pl Anatole France			•				•	
Viry Châtillon: le plateau			•					
Viry Châtillon: pl des Martyrs		•			•		•	
Yerres: centre ville			•		•			
Yerres: gare patinoires			•				•	

Department of Hauts de Seine								
Location	M	T	W	Th	F	S	Su	Comments
Antony: centre ville		•		•			•	
Antony: marché des Baconnets					•			
Asnieres: des Victoires				•			•	
Asnieres: marché de Bretagne			•		•			
Asnieres: marché de la République		•		•				
Asnieres: marché des 4 Routes				•			•	
Asnieres: marché des Mourinoux			•		•			
Asnieres: marché Flachat		•			•		•	
Bagneux: Albert Petit-Léo Ferret				•			•	
Bagneux: marché Dampierre		•		•				
Bois Colombes: des Chambards		•		•				
Bois Colombes: marché du centre	•		•		•			
Boulogne: Billancourt			•		•			
Boulogne: Biologique					•			1st & 3rd Saturday Organic foods
Boulogne: Escudier Jaures		•		•			•	
Boulogne: Pierre Grenier			•				•	
Boulogne: rue de Seine			•				•	Thursday 15.00-20.00
Bourg la Reine: marché Condorcet		•			•			
Chatenay Malabry: de la Butte Rouge			•				•	
Châtenay Malabry: marché du centre		•		•				
Châtillon: llot du marché		•		•			•	
Chaville: Municipal		•	•				•	
Clamart: de la Fourche		•					•	
Clamart: du Pavé Blanc			•				•	
Clamart: du Trosy		•			•			
Clichy: de Lorraine	•	•		•	•			
Clichy: marché du centre			•			•	•	
Colombes: de l'Europe			•		•	•		Friday evening
Colombes: du Petit Colombes		•			•		•	
Colombes: Marceau			•		•			
Colombes: marché du centre		•	•				•	
Courbevoie: Charras			•	•			•	
Courbevoie: Marceau			•		•			
Courbevoie: Villebois Mareuil			•		•			
Fontenay Aux Roses: de Verdun		•		•	•			
Garches: marché St-Louis			•		•			
Gennevilliers: des Grésillons			•		•			
Gennevilliers: marché du village		•			•		•	
Issy les Moulineaux: de la République			•	•				
Issy les Moulineaux: halles des Epinettes				•				
Issy les Moulineaux: marché Gambetta		•					•	
Issy les Moulineaux: Ste-Lucie			•	•				
La Garenne Colombes: centre			•		•			
La Garenne Colombes: des Vallées		•		•			•	
Le Plessis Robinson: marché de la Libération		•		•			•	
Levallois Perret: Barbusse		•		•			•	
Levallois Perret: de l'Europe					•			
Levallois Perret: de la Libération	•		•					
Levallois Perret: Jean Zay		•			•			

Location	M	T	W	Th	F	S	Su	Comments
Malakof: du Clos				•		•		
Malakof: pl du 11 Novembre			•		•		•	
Meudon: Bellevue			•		•			
Meudon: la Forêt	•				•		•	
Meudon: Maison Rouge	•				•		•	
Montrouge: centre				•			•	
Montrouge: de la Marne	•			•				
Montrouge: Jules Ferry		•				•		
Nanterre: Gare: av Benoit Frachon		•				•		
Nanterre: Picasso: pl de la Colombe		•				•		
Nanterre: pl du Maréchal Foch	•		•				•	
Neuilly: métro Sablons		•			•		•	
Neuilly: rue Windsor		•			•		•	
Puteaux: Rond Point des Bergères		•				•		
Puteaux: rue Eugène Eischenberger				•			•	
Rueil Malmaison: av de Colmar					•			
Rueil Malmaison: pl de l'Europe					•			
Rueil Malmaison: pl Henri Regnault	•				•			
Rueil Malmaison: pl Jean Jaures	•					•	•	Organic produce on Sundays
Rueil Malmaison: rue des Bons Raisins		•					•	
Sceaux: 66 rue Houdan		•			•			
Sceaux: av Jules Guesde							•	
Sèvres: marché St-Romain	•	•			•	•	•	
St-Cloud: bd. Senard				•			•	
St-Cloud: marché de Montretout		•			•			
Suresnes: pl du Général Leclerc		•			•			
Suresnes: pl Marcel Legras	•			•				
Suresnes: rue Albert Caron				•			•	
Vanves: rue Antoine Frattacci	•				•			
Vaucresson: pl du Marché				•			•	
Ville d'Avray: pl de l' Église	•				•		•	
Villeneuve la Garenne: rue Henri Barbusse	•				•		•	

Department of Seine St-Denis

Location	M	T	W	Th	F	S	Su	Comments
Aubervilliers		•	•	•	•	•	•	
Aubervilliers: marché du Centre		•			•			
Aulnay sous Bois: Marché de la Gare		•		•			•	
Aulnay sous Bois: Marché de la Mairie				•			•	
Bagnolet			•	•		•	•	
Bobigny		•	•	•		•	•	
Bondy		•	•	•		•	•	
Clichy sous Bois			•				•	
Drancy		•			•		•	
Dugny		•			•		•	
Epinay sur Seine			•	•	•	•	•	
Gagny		•	•	•	•	•	•	
Gournay sur Marne			•		•			
La Courneuve		•			•		•	
Le Blanc Mesnil: Marché de l' Aviation		•			•		•	

Location	M	T	W	Th	F	S	Su	Comments
Le Blanc Mesnil: Marché du Centre				•			•	
Le Bourget			•		•			
Le Pré St-Gervais		•		•	•			
Le Raincy: rond point de Montfermeil	•	•	•	•	•	•	•	
Les Lilas				•			•	
Les Pavillons sous Bois		•	•	•		•	•	
Livry Gargan		•	•	•		•	•	
Montfermeil		•	•	•	•	•	•	
Montreuil: bd Henri Barbusse				•			•	
Montreuil: bd Sueur			•		•			
Montreuil: pl de la République			•		•			
Montreuil: pl du Marché				•	•		•	Friday evening
Montreuil: rue des Roches		•		•				
Montreuil: rue du Jardin-École		•			•		•	
Montreuil: rue Paul Signac				•			•	
Neuilly Plaisance		•		•	•		•	
Neuilly sur Marne		•	•	•	•	•	•	
Noisy le Grand	•	•	•	•	•	•	•	
Noisy le Sec: pl de la Découverte	•		•	•			•	
Pantin		•	•	•	•	•	•	
Pierrefitte sur Seine				•	•			
Rosny sous Bois		•	•	•	•	•	•	
Sevran				•	•			
St-Denis		•			•		•	
St-Ouen	•					•	•	Monday all day
Stains			•		•			Saturday afternoon
Tremblay en France		•		•		•	•	
Villemomble		•	•	•	•	•		
Villepinte			•				•	

Department of Val de Marne

Location	M	T	W	Th	F	S	Su	Comments
Bry sur Marne			•				•	
Choisy le Roi				•			•	
Fontenay sous Blois: pl des Laures							•	Morning
Fontenay sous Blois: pl Doreau David			•	•	•	•	•	
Fontenay sous Blois: pl Roubleau				•	•	•	•	
Fontenay sous Blois: pl Verdun				•	•	•	•	Saturday afternoon
Joinville le Pont: av pellieui		•	•	•	•			
Joinville le Pont: pl du 8 Mai				•	•	•	•	
La Varenne St-Hilaire				•			•	
Le Perreux sur Marne			•		•		•	
Nogent sur Marne		•	•		•			
Vincennes: pl Carnot					•			
Vincennes: pl Diderot			•		•			
Vincennes: rue de Fontenay		•			•		•	

Department of Val d'Oise

Location	M	T	W	Th	F	S	Su	Comments
Argenteuil: av Stalingrad:		•		•		•		
Argenteuil: bd Gal Delambre			•			•		
Argenteuil: bd Héloïse					•		•	
Argenteuil: rue Rosière			•			•		
Auvers sur Oise: pl du Marché				•			•	
Avernes						•		
Beauchamp				•			•	
Beaumont sur Oise		•		•		•		
Bessancourt		•			•			
Bezons		•		•			•	
Bouffémont			•			•		
Butry sur Oise		•						
Cergy: St-Christophe			•			•		
Chars					•			
Cormeilles en Parisis			•			•		
Deuil la Barre			•		•			
Domont				•			•	
Eaubonne		•		•			•	
Écouen		•				•		
Enghien les Bains		•		•		•		
Ennery					•			
Éragny sur Oise			•	•		•	•	
Ermont			•			•		
Ézanville			•			•		
Fosses		•		•		•		
Franconville la Garenne			•	•		•	•	
Frépillon			•					
Garges lès Gonesse			•	•		•	•	
Gonesse		•	•	•	•	•	•	
Goussainville		•		•		•	•	
Groslay			•			•		
Herblay		•			•	•		
Jouy le Moutier						•		
L' Isle Adam: pl de Verdun		•			•		•	
L' Isle Adam: quart. De Nogent						•		Organic produce
La Frette sur Seine			•					
La Roche Guyon							•	
Le Plessis Bouchard			•			•		
Le Thillay					•			
Louvres			•				•	
Luzarches					•			
Magny en Vexin						•		
Marines		•				•		
Menucourt		•				•		
Méry sur Oise	•							
Montigny lès Cormeilles						•		
Montmagny		•		•		•	•	
Montmorency: centre ville	•	•			•	•	•	
Montsoult		•			•			

Location	M	T	W	Th	F	S	Su	Comments
Osny: quart. de la Gare							•	
Persan		•					•	
Pierrelaye			•				•	
Pontoise: Notre Dame			•					
Pontoise: pl de l' Hôtel de Ville					•			
Pontoise: quart de la Gare		•						Afternoon
Pontoise: quart. des Cordeliers	•			•				
Roissy en France					•			
Sannois	•		•				•	
Sarcelles	•	•		•	•	•		
Soisy sous Montmorency		•		•			•	
St-Brice sous Forêt	•							
St-Gratien		•					•	
St-Leu la Forêt		•			•			
St-Martin du Tertre							•	Thursday evening
St-Ouen L'Aumône: pl M.France		•					•	
Taverny	•			•				
Vallangoujard	•							Evening
Vauréal			•				•	
Viarmes		•			•			
Villiers le Bel	•	•		•	•	•		Tuesday, Thursday & Friday evening

DEPARTMENTS

Loire Atlantique	(44)
Maine et Loire	(49)
Mayenne	(53)
Sarthe	(72)
Vendée	(85)

Department of Loire Atlantique								
Location	M	T	W	Th	F	S	Su	Comments
Ancenis: pl de l'Eglise				•				
Arthon en Retz						•		Last Saturday
Asserac		•						July & August
Basse Goulaine			•					
Batz sur Mer	•				•			July & August
Blain		•	•	•	•	•		
Bouaye				•				
Bouguenais				•	•			
BourgneufenRetz					•			
Boussay	•	•	•	•	•	•	•	
Bouvron					•			
Campbon					•			
Carquefou				•				
Châteaubriant		•						
Chauve		•		•			•	
Clisson		•	•		•			
Corqoue sur Logne				•				1st Thursday
Couëron				•	•			
Derval					•			
Donges				•				
Frossay				•				
Geneston		•						3rd Wednesday
Grandchamp des Fontaines					•			
Guémené Penfao					•			
Guérande		•			•			
Haute Goulaine		•						
Herbignac		•						
Indre		•			•	•	•	
La Baule: av des Ibis	•	•	•	•	•	•	•	
La Bernerie en Retz	•				•			15th June to 30th September
La Chapelle Basse Mer							•	

Location	M	T	W	Th	F	S	Su	Comments
La Chapelle sur Erdre					●			
La Chevrolière			●					
La Haie Fouassière			●					
La Montagne			●					
La Plaine sur Mer							●	1st July to 31st August
La Turballe			●		●			
Le Cellier			●					
Le Clion sur Mer			●		●			Wednesday seasonal
Le Croisic	●		●		●			Monday July to August
Le Fresne sur Loire			●					
Le Landreau			●					1st Wednesday
Le Loroux Bottereau							●	
Le Pellerin					●			
Le Pouliguen	●	●	●	●	●	●	●	
Le Temple de Bretagne		●						
Legé		●					●	1st & 3rd Tuesday
Les Moutiers en Rietz				●		●		Saturday 15th June to end of August
Les Sorinieres				●				
Machecoul			●					
Mesquer		●			●			Friday 15th June to 15th September
Missillac			●					
Montoir de Bretagne	●							
Nantes: bd des Américains		●						
Nantes: bourg de St-Joseph de Porterie					●			
Nantes: Du Pont du Cens				●				
Nantes: Jean Macé		●						
Nantes: les Dervallières					●			
Nantes: pl de la Marrière				●				
Nantes: pl de la Petite Hollande					●			
Nantes: pl du Bouffay		●	●	●	●	●		
Nantes: pl du Ralliement		●						
Nantes: pl du Vieux Doulon							●	
Nantes: pl Ste-Anne				●				
Nantes: pl Viarme					●			
Nantes: pl Zola				●				
Nantes: Près du Centre Commercial		●						
Nantes: rue de Talensac		●	●	●	●	●	●	
Nantes: rue Esnoult des Châtelets		●						
Nort sur Erdre					●			
Nozay						●		
Orvault					●			
Paimboeuf		●			●			
Piriac: pl de l'Eglise	●	●			●			June - September
Pont St-Martin					●			
Pontchâteau: centre ville	●							All day
Pornic			●	●	●	●		
Pornichet		●			●			
Préfailles		●			●			Saturday 15th June to 15th September
Rezé		●		●		●		
Riaillé					●			1st & 3rd Saturday
Rougé	●							

Location	M	T	W	Th	F	S	Su	Comments
Sautron							•	
Savnay			•					
Sion les Mines		•						
St-Brévin les pins				•		•	•	
St-Étienne de Montluc					•			
St-Herblain		•	•		•			
St-Jean de Boiseau						•		
St-Joachim						•		
St-Julien de Concelles						•		
St-Lyphard				•			•	Sunday 30th June to 30th August
St-Malo de Guersac				•				
St-Mars du Desert							•	1st & 3rd Sunday
St-Mars la Jaille		•						
St-Michel Chef Chef		•	•		•	•		seasonal
St-Nazaire: Boulletterie			•					
St-Nazaire: centre		•			•		•	
St-Nazaire: Penhoët			•		•			
St-Nazaire: Perthischaud				•				
St-Nazaire: St-Marc sur Mer				•			•	
St-Père en Retz		•						1st & 3rd Tuesday
St-Philbert de Gd-Lieu							•	
St-Sébastien sur Loire		•		•	•			
Ste-Luce						•		
Ste-Pazanne				•				
Sucé sur Erdre		•			•			
Tharon		•			•			seasonal
Touvois	•							2nd & 4th Monday
Treillières				•				
Trignac			•	•	•	•		
Vallet							•	
Varades						•		
Vertou						•	•	
Vieillevigne						•		
Vigneux de Bretagne						•		
Vue							•	

Department of Maine et Loire

Location	M	T	W	Th	F	S	Su	Comments
Allonnes							•	
Angers: Belle Beille: pl la Dauversière				•				
Angers: Belle Beille: pl V Bernier		•						
Angers: Bichon			•					
Angers: Bordillon						•		
Angers: Grand Pigeon: bd des Deux Croix				•				
Angers: Jeanne d'Arc			•					
Angers: La Fayette		•				•		
Angers: La Roseraie						•		
Angers: Monplaisir: bd Allonneau		•				•		
Angers: pl Leclerc						•		
Angers: St-Laud						•		Organic produce

Location	M	T	W	Th	F	S	Su	Comments
Angers: Villesicard		•						
Avrillé		•						Afternoon
Avrille: Bois du Roy					•			
Baugé: pl du marché	•							Afternoon
Bauné					•			
Beaufort en Vallée				•				
Beaupréau: pl du 11 Novembre	•							
Brissac Quincé				•				
Candé: centre ville	•							
Chalonnes sur Loire		•				•		
Champigné		•						
Châteauneuf sur Sarthe					•			
Chemillé				•				
Cheviré le Rouge				•				
Cholet: Bretagne			•					
Cholet: Cité Laurient Bonnevay				•				
Cholet: le Chiron			•					
Cholet: Les Roches		•						
Cholet: Les Turbaudiéres		•						
Cholet: Nana et Travot			•					
Cholet: pl du 8 Mai					•			
Cholet: pl Rouget			•					
Cholet: Ste-Bernadette		•						
Combrée				•				
Combrée: Bel Air					•			
Corné		•						
Doué la Fontaine: pl de Verdun	•							
Fontevraud l'Abbaye			•					
Gennes		•						
Geste		•						
Ingrandes sur Loire					•			
Jallais					•			
La Ménitré					•			
La Pommeraye						•		
La Poueze		•						
Le Lion d'Angers					•			
Le Louroux Béconnais				•				
Le May sur Évre			•					
Le Vieil Bauge				•				
Les Points de Cé: La Chesnaie							•	
Les Points de Cé: pl Leclerc					•			
Les Rosiers: pl du Mail	•							
Longues Jumelles				•				
Martigné Briand						•		
Mazé				•				
Montevrault			•					
Montfaucon sur Moine		•						
Montjean sur Loire				•				
Montreuil Bellay		•						
Montreuil Juigné					•			
Montsoreau							•	

Location	M	T	W	Th	F	S	Su	Comments
Morannes				•				
Noyant					•			
Parcaye les Pins						•		
Pouancé				•				
Rochefort sur Loire			•					
Saumur: av du G.Gaulle				•				
Saumur: parking av Pompidou			•					
Saumur: pl Bilange						•		Flowers
Saumur: pl Chumeau Bagneux							•	
Saumur: pl de la République						•		
Saumur: pl St-Pierre						•		
Saumur: qrt du Chemin Vert				•				
Saumur: rue du Clos Grolleau			•					
Segré			•					
Seiches sur le Loir				•				
St-Barthélemy d'Anjou		•						
St-Crespin sur Moine	•		•					
St-Florent le Vieil					•			Afternoon
St-Georges sur Loire				•				
St-Germain sur Moine						•		
St-Lambert du Lattay			•					
St-Leger des Bois		•						
St-Macaire en Mauges				•				
St-Mathurin sur Loire		•						
St-Pierre Montlimart					•			
St-Remy la Varenne							•	
St-Sylvain d'Anjou							•	
Thouarcé		•						
Tiercé			•					
Torfou					•			Afternoon
Trélazé: Les plaines				•				
Trélazé: pl G.Péri							•	
Varennes sur Loire					•			
Vernantes			•					
Vihiers			•					
Villedieu la Blouère				•				

Department of Mayenne

Location	M	T	W	Th	F	S	Su	Comments
Ambrières: pl du Marché					•			
Andouillé: l'Eglise				•				
Bazouges							•	
Château Gontier				•				
Cossé le Vivien			•					
Craon	•							
Ernée		•						
Évron				•				
Fougerolles du Plessis					•			
Gorron			•					
Grez en Bouère		•						

Location	M	T	W	Th	F	S	Su	Comments
Javron					•			
Lassay		•						
Laval: centre		•				•		
Laval: Gare						•		
Laval: le Bourny			•					
Laval: Murat				•	•			
Laval: St-Nicholas				•			•	
Le Bourgneuf							•	
Mayenne: pl Clemenceau	•					•		
Meslay du Maine					•			
Montsûrs		•						
Port Brillet		•						
Pré en Pail					•			
Renazé					•			
St-Berthevin				•				
Villaines la Juhel: pl Neuve	•							

Department of Sarthe

Location	M	T	W	Th	F	S	Su	Comments
Allones: pl du Mail		•			•			
Arnage: pl de l'Église			•		•			
Aubigné Racan: pl de la Mairie					•			
Auvers le Hamon: pl de l'Églie		•						
Ballon: pl de la République			•					
Beauffay: pl de Général de Gaulle				•				
Beaumont sur Sarthe: pl des Halles		•						
Bessé sur Braye: Henri IV					•			
Bonnétable: pl du Marché		•		•				
Bouloire: pl du Château		•						Afternoon
Brette les Pins: pl des Acacias		•						All day
Brûlon: pl de la Mairie					•			
Cérans Foulletourte: pl Pierre Belon		•						
Champagné: pl de l' Église				•				
Changé: pl de l' Église			•					
Château du Loir: pl de l' Hotel de Ville			•					Textiles, clothes etc.
Château du Loir: pl des Halles					•			
Conlie: pl des Halles			•					
Connerré: pl de la République			•					
Coulaines: rue de la Paix			•		•			
Coulans sur Gée: pl de l' Église		•						
Coulongé: pl de l' Église		•						All day
Cré sur Loir: pl de l' Église				•				
Dollon: pl de l' Église			•					
Écommoy: pl de la République		•						
Guécélard: pl Dugué							•	
Jupilles: pl Ricordeau							•	
L' Homme: pl Albert Etiembre		•						
La Chapelle d'Aligné: pl de l' Église				•				
La Chartre sur le Loir: parking central			•					
La Ferté Bernard: pl de la République	•							

Location	M	T	W	Th	F	S	Su	Comments
La Flèche: bvd Maréchal Foch			•					All day
La Flèche: pl de la Libération			•					All day
La Fresnay sur Sarthe: rue de Fres.sur Sarthe					•			
La Suze sur Sarthe: centre Bourg				•				
Laigné en Belin: pl de la Chanterie				•				
Le Grand Lucé: pl de la République			•					All day
Le Luart: pl de l'Église							•	
Le Lude: pl Neuve				•				
Le Mans: Av de Paderborn			•		•		•	
Le Mans: Av Jean Jaures					•			
Le Mans: Citè des Maillets		•						
Le Mans: Citè des Pins					•			
Le Mans: Citè des Sablons				•				
Le Mans: Cites des Bruyéres					•			
Le Mans: Epau		•						
Le Mans: Gautrie				•				
Le Mans: Gazonfier		•			•			
Le Mans: Il Lecornué					•			
Le Mans: Patis St-Lazare					•			
Le Mans: pl des Jacobins					•			All day
Le Mans: pl du Jet d'Eau			•		•		•	
Le Mans: pl Edouard de la Boussinière		•						
Le Mans: pl Henri Vaillant			•				•	
Le Mans: qtr St-Julien: Z.I.S		•		•	•			
Le Mans: rue Bobillot				•				
Le Mans: rue Hippolyte Lecornué					•			
Loué: pl Albert Etiembre		•						
Luché Pringé: pl du monument		•						
Malicorne sur Sarthe: pl de la République				•				
Mamers: pl Carnot	•							All day
Mansigné: pl de la Mairie	•							
Marolles les Braults: pl de l' Église				•				
Mayet: pl de l'Hotel de Ville							•	
Montaillé: pl de l' Église							•	Every fifteen days
Montfort le Gesnois: av de la Libération					•			
Mulsanne: pl Jeanne Moulin					•			
Nogent le Bernard: pl de l' Église			•				•	
Noyen sur Sarthe: pl de la République					•			
Parcé sur Sarthe: pl de la République				•				
Parigné L'Eveque: pl de l'Eglise				•	•			
Pontvallain: bvd Dubois Lecordier					•			
Précigné: rue Abbé Louis Chevallier					•			
Requeil: pl du 8 mai 1945					•			
Sablé sur Sarthe: pl de la République	•							
Sablé sur Sarthe: pl Raphaël Elizé					•			2nd Saturday all day
Sarge les Le Mans: pl de la Poste		•						
Savigné L'Évêque: pl de Gaulle					•			
Sillé le Guillaume: pl de la Gare			•					
Sillé le Guillaume: pl de la République			•					
Sillé le Guillaume: pl St-Etienne			•		•			
St-Aubin des Coudray: pl de l' Église							•	

Location	M	T	W	Th	F	S	Su	Comments
St-Calais: Centre ville				•				All day
St-Come en Vairais: pl de la Bascule						•		
St-Georges le Gaultier: pl de l'Église		•						
St-Maixent: pl de l' Église		•						Afternoon
Telloché: pl du Docteur Alain			•					
Tresson: pl du Village				•				
Tuffé: pl de Général Leclerc			•					
Vaas: pl de l' Église		•						
Vancé: pl St-Martin		•						
Vibraye: pl de l' Église				•				
Yvré L'Évêque: rue de Touraine						•		
Yvré le Polin: pl de l' Église				•				

Department of Vendée

Location	M	T	W	Th	F	S	Su	Comments
Aizenay	•							1st & 3rd Monday
Avrille				•				2nd Thursday
Beauvoir sur Mer				•				
Bournezeau		•						1st Tuesday
Bretignolles sur Mer				•			•	Thursday seasonal
Challans		•						
Chantonnay		•						2nd & 4th Tuesday
Coex					•			
Fontenay le Comte					•			
Fromentine					•			seasonal
Jard sur Mer: pl des Ormeaux	•							
L' Aiguillon sur Mer		•		•				
L' Hebergement			•					seasonal
La Châtaigneraie	•							4th Monday
La Faute sur Mer				•			•	seasonal
La Ferriere					•			1st Friday
La Mothe Achard				•	•			1st Thursday
La Roche sur Yon	•	•		•		•		
La Tranche sur Mer		•			•			
Les Essarts			•					3rd Wednesday
Les Herbiers				•	•			2nd Thursday & last Wednesday
Les Sables d'Olonne: bd Arago		•	•	•	•	•	•	Flowers & outdoor market Tuesday, Friday & Sunday
Les Sables d'Olonne: Cours du Pont			•		•			
Les Sables d'Olonne: La Chaume		•		•	•		•	Friday flowers July & August
Les Sables d'Olonne: les Halles		•	•	•	•	•	•	Local produce from surrounding co-operatives
Les Sables d'Olonne: que Franqueville		•	•	•	•	•	•	Fish
Longeville: pl de l'Eglise	•							1st & 3rd Monday
Luçon					•			
Mareuil sur Lay				•				4th Thursday
Montaigu			•	•				2nd Wednesday & last Thursday
Moutiers les Mauxfaits	•							Last Monday
Nieul le Dolent		•						4th Tuesday
Noirmoutier en L' Ile		•		•			•	Sunday & Tuesday in season
Notre Dame de Monts							•	
Poiré sur Vie			•					1st & 3rd Thursday

Location	M	T	W	Th	F	S	Su	Comments
Pouzauges				•				
Sion St-Hilaire		•			•			seasonal
St-Gilles Croix de Vie		•	•	•		•	•	
St-Hilaire de Riez: les Mouettes				•			•	Daily in season
St-Jean de Monts			•			•		Daily in season
St-Michel en L' Herm				•				seasonal
Ste-Hermine					•			
Talmont St-Hilaire				•				3rd Thursday

DEPARTMENTS

Aisne	(2)
Oise	(60)
Somme	(80)

Department of Aisne								
Location	M	T	W	Th	F	S	Su	**Comments**
Bohain en Vermandois					•			
Charly sur Marne				•				
Château Thierry					•			
Chauny		•			•			
Coincy L' Abbaye							•	2nd Sunday April to October
Condé en Brie								1st Sunday April to October
Fargniers							•	
Fère en Tardenois				•				
Ferme de la Genevroye					•			2nd Saturday all day for organic products
Fresnoy le Grand: pl du General de Gaulle	•							
Guise					•			1st Thursday
Hirson: pl Victor Hugo	•				•			Thursday at pl de République
Laon: pl d' Ardon							•	Local produce lower part of town
Laon: pl de l'Hôtel de Ville			•					Upper part of town
Laon: pl Marché aux Herbes					•			Upper part of town
Laon: pl Victor Hugo-Pont de Vaux			•					
Laon: qrt Champagne	•				•			Afternoons in lower part of town
Laon: qrt Montreuil	•							lower part of town
Le Nouvion en Thiérache			•					
Marigny en Orxois							•	Last Sunday from April to October
Marle		•						2nd Tuesday
Origny Ste-Benoîte			•					
Rocourt St-Martin					•			2nd Saturday all day for organic products
Soissons			•		•			
St-Quentin			•		•			Also Saturday evening at quartier Chamoagne
Vailly sur Aisne							•	
Vervins					•			
Vic sur Aisne			•					
Villers Cotterêts					•			

Department of Oise

Location	M	T	W	Th	F	S	Su	Comments
Andeville: pl de l' Église					•			Afternoon
Auneuil: pl de la Folie							•	
Baron: pl Jeanne d' Arc	•							
Beauvais: av de l'Europe				•				
Beauvais: pl de France Zup	•							
Beauvais: pl des Halles			•		•			
Béthisy St-Pierre: pl du marché				•				
Bornel: pl de l' Eglise					•			
Bresles: pl du 11 Novembre				•				
Chambly: pl ChArles de Gaulle			•		•			
Chantilly: pl St-Omer Vallon			•		•			
Chaumont en Vexin: allée St-Nicolas					•			
Chevrières: pl des Chevrières							•	
Cires les Mello: pl de l' Église				•				
Clermont: pl de l' Hôtel de Ville					•			
Compiègne: pl du Change			•					
Compiégne: pl du Marché					•			
Coye la Forêt: pl des Rivaux		•			•			
Creil: Champs de Mars				•				
Creil: pl Carnot			•		•			
Crepy en Valois: av Kennedy							•	
Crépy en Valois: pl de la République			•					
Crèvecoeur le Grand: pl de l' Hôtel de Ville			•					Afternoon
Crevecoeur le Grand: pl du 7 Juin 1940							•	Local Produce
Cuise la Motte: pl du Marché							•	
Estrées St-Denis: pl du Marché		•						Afternoon
Fitz James: pl de la République				•				
Fleurines: pl de l' Église							•	
Formerie: pl Centrale			•				•	Wednesday afternoon
Gouvieux: pl de la Mairie			•				•	
Grandvilliers: pl Barbier	•							Afternoon
Guiscard: pl de Magny			•				•	
Hermes: pl de l' Église							•	
Lamorlaye: Allée des Arcades					•			
Lamorlaye: pl du 8 Mai		•						
Le Plessis Brion: pl Bobigny		•						
Liancourt: pl Rochefoucault			•					
Longueil Annel: av du G.Gaulle				•				
Margny les Compiegne: pl de la République		•		•				
Marseille en Beauvaisis: pl Warnault				•				
Méru: pl de l' Hôtel de Ville				•			•	
Montataire: pl de la Mairie			•				•	
Mouy: pl de l' Hôtel de Ville					•			Afternoon
Nanteuil le Haudouin: pl de la Mairie			•					Afternoon
Neuilly en Thelle: pl T.Lefebvre				•				
Noailles: pl du Mardi							•	
Nogent sur Oise: pl Burton				•				
Noyon: pl de l' Hôtel de Ville		•			•			1st Tuesday
Orry la Ville: pl de la Libération			•		•			Saturday afternoon

Location	M	T	W	Th	F	S	Su	Comments
Pierrefonds: pl de l' Hôtel de Ville					•			
Plailly: pl de l' Église				•			•	
Pont Ste-Maxence: pl champs de Mar		•			•			Friday at pl General Leclerc
Rantigny: pl de la République					•			Afternoon
Ribécourt Dreslincourt: pl de la République					•			
Senlis: centre ville		•			•			
Sérifontaine: rue Alexandré Barbier						•		
St-Just en Chaussée		•						
St-Leu d'Esserent: pl de la République				•				Evening
Ste-Geneviève: pl de la Mairie				•				
Thourotte: pl de la République				•				
Verberie: pl du G.Gaulle				•				
Verneuil en Balatte: pl de l' Église					•			Afternoon
Villers St-Paul: pl Arthur du Thilleul				•		•		Thursday evening
Villers St-Paul: pl du Marché						•		
Vineuil St-Firmin: pl d' Aumale				•				
Warluis: pl Communale		•			•			

Department of Somme

Location	M	T	W	Th	F	S	Su	Comments
Abbeville			•	•	•			All day last Wednesday of the month
Ailly le Haut Clocher						•		2nd & 4th Saturday
Ailly sur Noye			•					
Albert			•		•			2nd Wednesday
Amiens: Marché à Etouvie					•			
Amiens: Marché à l' Esplanade Branly				•				
Amiens: Marché de Prague rue Pierre Rollin		•			•			Friday afternoon
Amiens: Marché du Colvert							•	
Amiens: pl au Fil			•		•			All day
Amiens: pl Parmentier				•	•			Local produce market held on the river
Araines					•		•	Friday afternoon & alternate Sundays
Athies			•					
Ault: pl de l' Eglise					•			
Bray sur Somme			•					1st Wednesday
Cayeaux sur Mer		•			•		•	Sunday seasonal
Chaulnes			•					
Combles							•	1st Sunday
Conty					•			
Corbie					•			
Crécy en Ponthieu: rue de Mal Leclerc	•							
Doullens				•				
Fort Mahon Plage		•			•			15th June to 15th September
Friville Escarbotin						•		
Gamaches			•		•			1st Wednesday
Ham						•		
Le Crotoy		•			•			15th June to 15th September
Le Crotoy: pl Jeanne d' Arc					•			seasonal
Mers les Bains: pl du marché	•			•				
Montdidier				•				
Moreuil		•						

Location	M	T	W	Th	F	S	Su	Comments
Oisemont						•		
Onival: rue St-Valery			•					seasonal
Péronne			•			•		
Picquigny							•	Alternate Sundays
Poix de Picardie							•	
Quend Plage	•			•				Monday seasonal
Roye					•		•	1st Sunday
Rue: pl de Verdun					•			
St-Valery sur Somme: pl des pilotes							•	
St-Valery sur Somme: pl du jeu de battoir			•					seasonal
Villers Brettonneux			•					
Villers Garth			•					

DEPARTMENTS

Charente	(16)
Charente Maritime	(17)
Deux Sèvres	(79)
Vienne	(86)

Department of Charente

Location	M	T	W	Th	F	S	Su	Comments
Aigre				•		•	•	
Angoulême: Basseau: pl du marché		•		•				
Angoulême: Marché Victor Hugo		•	•	•	•	•	•	
Angoulême: pl Felix Gaillard		•		•				
Angoulême: pl Mulac	•			•		•		Monday & Thursday afternoons
Angoulême: pl St-Jacques		•			•			
Baignes Ste-Radegonde			•					4th Wednesday
Barbezieux: pl de l'Eglise		•			•			
Blanzac Porcheresse					•			1st Saturday
Brossac					•			2nd & 4th Saturday
Chabanais				•				1st Thursday
Chalais	•							
Champagne Mouton		•			•			
Champniers					•			
Chaseneuil sur Bonnieure			•		•			
Châteauneuf sur Charente		•		•	•			
Cognac	•	•	•	•	•	•	•	
Confolens			•		•			
Fleac: pl du Centre Commercial							•	
Gond Pontouvre: Av Jean-Sëbire				•				
Gond Pontouvre: Av Kennedy							•	
Isle d'Espagnac: pl Francois Mittérand		•			•			
Jarnac: des Halles		•	•	•	•	•	•	
La Couronne: pl de l'Hotel de Ville		•						Afternoon
La Couronne: pl du Champ de Foire					•			
La Rochefoucauld			•		•			
Magnac sur Touvre: pl de l'Union					•			
Mansle		•			•			
Montbron		•			•	•		
Montemboeuf			•					
Montignac Charente			•			•	•	

Location	M	T	W	Th	F	S	Su	Comments
Mouthiers Sur Boeme: pl de l' Église							•	
Mouthiers Sur Boeme: pl du Champ de foire			•					
Nersac: pl de l'Union			•				•	
Puymoyen: pl Genainville							•	
Rouillac		•			•			
Roullet St-Estèphe: pl de l' Église		•		•				
Ruelle sur Trouvre: pl Montalembert				•			•	
Ruffec		•		•	•			
Segonzac							•	
Soyaux: pl Jean Jacques Rousseau			•	•			•	
Soyaux: pl Lucien Petit		•		•				
St-Michel: av de la Republique		•		•				
Villebois Lavalette				•				
Villefagnan		•		•				

Department of Charente Maritime

Location	M	T	W	Th	F	S	Su	Comments
Aigrefeuille d'Aunis		•				•		2nd Tuesday
Angoulins sur Mer	•	•	•	•	•	•	•	
Archiac				•		•		1st Thursday
Ars en Ré	•	•	•	•	•	•	•	
Arvert: centre			•					
Aulnay de Saintonge: pl A.Briand	•						•	4th Monday
Authon Ebéon	•							3rd Monday
Aytré: pl des Grands Près				•				
Beauvais sur Matha		•		•				
Bedenac			•					3rd Wednesday
Bords				•				
Bourcefranc le Chapus			•		•		•	
Brie sous Mertagne		•						2nd Tuesday
Brizambourg			•					4th Wednesday
Burie				•				3rd Thursday
Cercoux				•				4th Thursday
Champagnolles		•						4th Tuesday
Chaniers			•					
Châtelaillon Plage: bd de la Libération	•	•	•	•	•	•	•	
Chérac				•				4th Thursday
Chevanceaux	•							2nd & 4th Monday
Corme Royal	•							4th Monday
Courçon d' Aums			•					
Cozes			•					
Dolus d'Oléron	•	•	•	•	•	•	•	Daily July - August
Dompierre sur Mer		•		•				
Échillais			•					
Épargnes				•				seasonal
Étaules		•						1st Tuesday
Fouras: esp du Sémaphore	•	•	•	•	•	•	•	
Gémozac				•				
Jarnac Champagne				•				Last Thursday
Jonzac: pl du marchlé		•		•				

Location	M	T	W	Th	F	S	Su	Comments
La Brée les Bains: pl des Ardilliéres			•		•			Daily in season
La Couarde sur Mer		•		•		•		Seasonal
La Flotte en Ré	•	•	•	•	•	•	•	
La Jarrie				•				
La Rochelle: pl du marché	•	•	•	•	•	•	•	
La Ronde				•				
La Tremblade					•			Daily in season
Le Bois Plage en Ré				•		•		Daily in season.
Le Château d'Oléron		•	•	•	•	•	•	
Léoville							•	Last Sunday
Les Mathes					•			Daily in season
Les Portes en Ré	•	•	•	•	•	•	•	Daily in season
Loix en Ré	•		•	•		•	•	July to August
Lonzac		•						3rd Wednesday
Lorignac	•							2nd Monday
Loulay				•				
Marans		•			•			
Marennes		•		•	•			
Marsilly			•		•			
Matha		•			•	•	•	
Mérignac					•			1st Saturday
Meschers	•	•	•	•	•	•	•	Daily June - September. Tuesday in winter
Mirambeau					•			
Montendre				•				
Montguyon			•		•			1st & 3rd Wednesday
Montils		•						2nd Tuesday
Montlieu la Garde			•					2nd Wednesday
Mornac sur Seudre			•					
Mosnac		•						1st Tuesday
Néré				•				1st
Nieul le Virouil					•			3rd Saturday
Nieul sur Mer							•	
Nieul sur Seudre				•				
Pérignac					•			4th Friday
Pisany								29th Livestock
Pons			•		•			
Pont l'Abbé: d'Arnoult				•				
Port d'Envaux				•				
Port des Barques	•	•	•	•	•	•	•	
Rioux		•						
Rivedoux Plage	•		•		•			June - Spetember
Rochefort sur Mer: av de Gaulle		•		•	•			
Royan			•				•	
Saintes		•	•	•	•	•	•	
Saujon		•			•			2nd Monday
St-Agnant				•				
St-Aiguilin				•				3rd Thursday
St-Bonnet sur Gironde	•							Last Monday
St-Christophe				•				
St-Ciers du Taillon		•						3rd Tuesday
St-Clément des Baleines	•	•	•	•	•	•	•	Daily in season

Location	M	T	W	Th	F	S	Su	Comments
St-Denis d'Oléron: G. de Gaulle	•	•	•	•	•	•	•	May - September
St-Dizant du Gua			•					3rd Wednesday
St-Fort sur Gironde						•	•	
St-Genis de Saintonge				•				
St-Georges d'Oléron: rue du marché					•			Daily in season
St-Georges de Didonne: rue Marché		•	•	•	•	•		
St-Georges des Coteaux			•					
St-Jean d'Angély			•					
St-Martin de Ré		•		•				
St-Palais sur Mer	•	•	•	•	•	•		June - September
St-Pierre d'Oléron: rue commerciale	•	•	•	•	•	•	•	
St-Porchaire			•					
St-Sauveur d'Aunis			•					
St-Savinien					•			
St-Sulpice de Royan			•					
St-Thomas de Conac	•							1st Monday
St-Trojan les Bains: pl des Filles de la Sagesse	•	•	•	•	•	•		
St-Xandre		•						
Ste-Marie de Ré: pl Antioche	•	•	•	•	•	•	•	
Surgères		•		•		•		
Taillebourg				•				
Tesson	•							4th Monday
Thairé d' Aums		•						
Thors		•						
Tonnay Boutonne			•					3rd Wednesday
Tonnay Charente			•			•		
Vaux sur Mer: pl F.Courtot		•	•	•	•	•	•	
Villeneuve la Comtesse					•			1st Friday

Department of Deux Sèvres

Location	M	T	W	Th	F	S	Su	Comments
Airvault: pl St-Pierre						•		
Argenton Château: pl de la Mairie				•				
Bressuire		•				•		Livestock fair on Tuesdays
Brioux sur Boutonne				•				2nd & 4th Thursday
Celles sur Belle			•					
Cerizay						•		
Champdeniers St-Denis						•		
Chef Boutonne						•		
Chizé		•						3rd Wednesday
Coulon					•		•	
Coulonges sur l'Autize		•						
La Crèche		•						
La Mothe St-Héray				•				
Les Aubiers				•				
Lezay		•						
Magné						•		
Mauléon				•				
Mauzé sur le Mignon			•			•		
Melle				•				

Location	M	T	W	Th	F	S	Su	Comments
Moncoutant						•		
Niort		•		•		•		
Nueil sur Argent						•		
Pamproux	•							
Parthenay			•					Livestock
Sauzé Vaussais				•				
Secondigny		•						
St-Loup Lamairé							•	
St-Maixent l'École			•		•			
Thénezay							•	
Thouars		•			•			
Vasles		•						

Department of Vienne

Location	M	T	W	Th	F	S	Su	Comments
Angles sur l'Anglin							•	
Archigny		•						Every 3rd week
Availles en Châtellerault					•			
Availles Limouzine								17th
Beaumont					•			
Bignoux					•			Afternoon
Bonneuil MaTours					•			Also 4th Tuesday
Brigueil le Chantre					•			Last Friday
Buxerolles			•					
Charroux			•					
Chasseneuil du Poitou			•					
Château Garnier								22nd
Châtellerault		•		•		•		Tuesday at bd Blossac
Chaunay	•							
Chauvigny		•		•		•		2nd Tuesday
Civaux			•		•			
Civray		•						1st
Couhé			•	•				2nd Wednesday & 1st,3rd & 4th Thursday
Dangé St-Romain		•			•			
Dissay				•	•			
Fontaine le Comte							•	
Gençay				•	•			
Iteuil					•			
Jaunay Clan					•			
L' Hommaize							•	2nd Sunday
L' Isle Jourdain					•			
La Roche Posay		•						
La Villedieu du Clain		•						
Latillé	•							
Lencloître					•			
Liguge			•					
Loudun		•						
Lusignan			•					
Lussac les Châteaux					•			
Migne Auxances						•		

Location	M	T	W	Th	F	S	Su	Comments
Mirebeau			•			•		
Moncontour						•	•	3rd Saturday
Montmorillon			•			•		
Monts sur Guesnes						•		
Naintre							•	
Neuville de Poitou				•			•	
Oyre			•					1st Wednesday
Persac			•					2nd Wednesday
Poitiers: Bel Air: Bellejouanne					•			
Poitiers: Bel Air: rue Magenta					•			Afternoon
Poitiers: Clos Gaultier				•				
Poitiers: pl Notre Dame					•			
Poitiers: pl Notre Dame Bellejouanne		•						
Poitiers: Zup des Couronneries			•				•	
Pressac			•					
Roches Premaries Andille					•			
Romagne							•	1st
Rouillé					•			
Saires						•	•	
Smarves					•			
Sommieres du Clain							•	
Sossay							•	
St-Benoît					•			
St-Gervais les Trois Clochers					•			
St-Jean de Sauves					•			1st Friday
St-Julien l 'Ars				•				
St-Savin					•			
Vendeuvre		•						
Vicq sur Gartempe					•			
Vivonne		•			•			
Vouillé					•			
Voulon							•	Local produce last Sunday in the month
Weneill				•				

DEPARTMENTS

Alpes de Haute Provence	(4)
Hautes Alpes	(5)
Alpes Maritimes	(6)
Bouches du Rhône	(13)
Var	(83)
Vaucluse	(84)

Department of Alpes de Haute Provence								
Location	M	T	W	Th	F	S	Su	Comments
Allemagne en Provence				•				
Allos: la Foux d'Allos				•				
Allos: Station de la Foux			•					
Annot: pl du Revely		•						
Banon: pl du marché		•						
Barcelonnette: pl Aimé Gassier			•		•			
Barrême	•							
Castellane			•		•			
Céreste				•				
Champtercier							•	
Château Arnoux: St-Auban							•	
Colmars les Alps: pl de la Tours		•			•			
Digne Les Bains			•		•			
Entrevaux					•			
Esparron de Verdon		•			•			
Forcalquier: centre ville	•							
Gréoux les Bains		•		•				
Jausiers							•	
L' Escale			•					
La Brillanne	•							
La Motte du Claire				•				
La Palud sur Verdon			•					
Les Mées		•			•			
Malijai				•				
Mallemoisson				•				
Mane							•	
Manosque					•			
Mezel					•			
Montagnac Montpezat					•			
Montclar							•	
Moustiers Ste-Marie				•				

Location	M	T	W	Th	F	S	Su	Comments
Oraison: centre ville		•						
Peyruis					•			
Pierrevert			•					
Quinson					•			
Reillanne				•			•	
Revest du Bion					•			
Riez			•		•			
Roumoules			•		•			
Seyne les Alpes: pl d'Armes		•			•			
Sisteron			•		•			
St-André les Alpes			•		•			
St-Étienne les Orgues			•		•			
St-Martin de Bromes		•						
St-Michel l'Observatoire							•	
St-Vincent sur Jabro							•	Mid July to September
Ste-Croix du Verdon		•						
Ste-Tulle			•					
Thoard							•	June to September
Uvernet Fours	•							
Valensole			•			•		2nd Wednesday
Villeneuve				•				
Volonne					•			
Volx		•						

Department of Hautes Alpes

Location	M	T	W	Th	F	S	Su	Comments
Abriès			•					
Aiguilles				•				
Aspres sur Buëch					•			
Baratier				•				Evening seasonal
Briançon: La Schappe			•					
Briançon: pl d' Armes		•						
Ceillac				•				
Châteauroux							•	
Chorges			•				•	Wednesday evening in summer Sunday seasonal
Embrun			•		•			
Gap: pl de la Republique			•					
Gap: pl Jean Marcellin					•			
Guillestre	•							Small market in winter
L' Argentière la Bessée					•			
La Chapelle en Valgaudem		•						Summer
La Grav				•				seasonal
La Roche des Arnauds					•			
La Saulce					•			
Laragne Montéglin				•				
Le Monétier les Bains					•			
Molines en Queyras		•						
Orcières				•				Summer & winter
Ribiers		•						Summer

Location	M	T	W	Th	F	S	Su	Comments
Rosans							•	
Savines: Pl des Commerces		•			•			
Serres						•		
St-Bonnet: av du 11 Novembre	•							
St-Étienne en Dévoluy					•			seasonal
St-Firmin		•						
Tallard		•			•			
Vallouise				•				
Vars		•						
Veynes				•				

Department of Alpes Maritimes

Location	M	T	W	Th	F	S	Su	Comments
Antibes: Cours Masséna		•	•	•	•	•	•	
Beaulieu sur Mer	•	•	•	•	•	•		Large market on Saturday
Beausoleil: bd de la République	•	•	•	•	•	•	•	
Beausoleil: bd des Moneghetti	•	•	•	•	•	•	•	
Cagnes sur Mer: Cité Marchande		•	•	•	•	•	•	
Cannes: marché Forville		•	•	•	•	•	•	In winter
Cap d'Ail				•				
Carros			•		•			
Drap					•			
Golfe Juan				•				
Grasse: cours Honoré Crest	•	•	•	•	•	•	•	
La Colle sur Loup					•			
La Trinité		•			•			
Le Cannet: pl de l'Aubarède, Villa Do Conde			•					Organic produce
Le Cannet: pl Foch							•	
Le Cannet: pl Jean Jaurès		•						
Mandelieu la Napoule: park des Termes			•					
Mandelieu la Napoule: pl des Mimosas					•			Last Friday
Mandelieu le Napoule: Capitou							•	Including organic produce
Menton	•	•	•	•	•	•	•	
Monaco: les halles St-Charles	•	•	•	•	•	•	•	All day
Monaco: pl d' Armes	•	•	•	•	•	•	•	
Mouans Sartoux: pl des Anciens Combattants		•						
Mouans Sartoux: pl Jean Jaurès				•				
Nice: bd Paul Montel		•				•		Clothes
Nice: bd St-Roch			•			•		
Nice: cours Saleya		•	•	•	•	•	•	All day except for food
Nice: pl de l'Ariane		•				•		Clothes
Nice: pl St-Francois		•	•	•	•	•	•	Fish
Nice: stade du Ray			•			•		Clothes
Pégomas					•			
Peymeinade	•							
Puget Theniers: pl Principale							•	
Roquebrune Cap Martin	•	•	•	•	•	•		
Sospel: pl des Platanes				•				Local produce
Sospel: pl du Marché							•	Local produce
St-Étienne de Tinée					•			

Location	M	T	W	Th	F	S	Su	Comments
St-Laurent du Var: prom des Flots Bleus						•		
St-Paul		•		•		•		
Tende			•					
Theoule sur Mer					•			
Valbonne: pl des Arcades		•		•	•			
Vallauris		•	•	•				
Vence: pl du Grand Jardin		•	•	•	•	•	•	Flowers
Vence: pl Surian		•						
Villefranche sur Mer: Jardin Binon						•		Traditional market
Villeneuve Loubet: village			•			•		

Department of Bouches du Rhône

Location	M	T	W	Th	F	S	Su	Comments
Aix en Provence: Cours Mirabeau		•		•			•	Jumble
Aix en Provence: pl de la Mairie	•	•		•		•		Flowers. Books & Antiques 1st Monday
Aix en Provence: pl de Madeleine		•		•	•			
Aix en Provence: pl des prechêurs	•	•		•			•	Flowers
Aix en Provence: pl Jeanne d'Arc	•							Bric-a-brac
Aix en Provence: pl Richelme	•	•	•	•	•	•	•	
Aix en Provence: pl Verdun		•		•	•			Bric-a-brac
Allauch: Cours de 11 Novembre			•					
Alleins: place de la République		•						
Arles			•		•			
Arles: bd des Lices			•		•			Bric-a-Brac 1st Wednesday
Arles: bd Emile Combes			•					
Arles: Mas Thibert: centre ville						•		
Arles: Raphele les Arles: centre ville		•						
Arles: Salin de Giraud: centre ville					•			
Aubagne: Cours Foch					•			Friday evening
Aubagne: Cours Foch, Esp De Gaulle		•						
Aubagne: Cours Voltaire		•		•	•	•		
Aubagne: pl Jean Rau					•			
Aureille: pl de la Fontaine			•					
Auriol: Cours du 4 Sept.			•		•			
Barbentane: Cours J.B.Rey				•				
Berre l'Étang: av. Paul Langevin		•						
Berre l'Étang: Bd Romain Rolland			•					
Berre l'Étang: pl de la Mairie						•		
Bouc Bel Air: pl Jean Moulin				•		•		
Boulbon: pl Gilles Léontin	•							
Cabannes: pl de la Mairie		•						
Cabannes: rue Ancienne Mairie					•			
Cadolive: pl de la Mairie			•					
Carnoux: Esplanade Liautey			•		•			
Carry le Rouet: pl du Marché		•			•			
Cassis: pl Baragnon			•		•			
Ceyreste: pl de la Mairie					•			
Charleval: Cours de la République					•			
Châteauneuf le Rouge: pl. Auguste Barret			•					Afternoon
Châteauneuf les Martigues: La Mède		•						

Location	M	T	W	Th	F	S	Su	Comments
Châteaurenard: centre ville	•	•	•	•	•	•	•	Daily in season
Corsy		•		•		•		
Coudoux: Centre commercial		•						
Coutheron		•						
Cuges les Pins: pl Léonard Blanc			•					
Éguilles: pl de la Poste		•		•				
Encagnane: pl Romée de Villeneuve	•		•		•		•	
Ensuès la Redonne: centre du village				•				
Eygalières: pl Marcel Bonein				•				
Eyguières: pl des Frères Roche		•						
Eyragues: pl de la Libération				•				
Fontvieille: Allées des pins	•			•				
Fos sur Mer: av Réne Cassin				•				
Fos sur Mer: pl de la République			•					
Fos sur Mer: pl du marché					•			
Fos sur Mer: Plage				•				July & August
Fos sur Mer: Qu. Du Pont du Roy				•				July & August
Fuveau: Cours Leydet	•			•				
Gardanne: Biver				•				
Gardanne: centre ville			•		•		•	
Gémenos: Cours Pasteur							•	
Gignac la Nerthe: pl de la Mairie							•	
Grans: place Jean Jaurès				•				
Gravson: Cours National				•				Afternoon daily in season
Gréasque: Cours Ferrer		•		•				
Istres: centre ville		•						
Istres: Entressen centre ville				•				
Istres: Rassuen, Prépaou				•				
Jas de bouffan: place la Croix Verte		•					•	
Jouques: pl des Anciens Comb.							•	
La Bouilladisse: pl de la Libération			•					
La Ciotat: pl Evariste Gras		•			•			
La Ciotat: Vieux Port	•	•	•	•	•	•	•	Evening except Sunday
La Destrousse: pl de la Mairie				•				
La Fare les Oliviers: Cours ChArles Gall					•			
La Penne sur Huveaune: pl. J.Pellegrin			•					
La Roque d'Anthéron: Cours Foch			•					
Lambesc: pl des états généraux		•		•			•	Tuesday evening
Lançon Provence: pl du Champ de Mars		•						
Le Paradou: pl de la Mairie		•						
Le Puy Ste-Réparade: centre ville							•	
Les Milles: Cours Brémond	•							
Luynes: pl de la Mairie	•							
Maillane: pl de l' Église			•					
Mallemort: pl Raoul Coustet				•				
Marignane: centre ville		•			•			
Marignane: pl du 11 Novembre			•					
Marseille:(01) Cours Joseph Thierry	•		•		•	•		
Marseille:(01) La Canebière		•			•			Flowers
Marseille:(01) pl de Capucins	•	•	•	•	•	•	•	All day
Marseille:(01) quai des Belges	•	•	•	•	•	•	•	Fish

Location	M	T	W	Th	F	S	Su	Comments
Marseille:(01) rue Bernard du Bois	•	•	•	•	•	•	•	fairs & entertainers all day
Marseille:(01) rue Halles Delacroix	•	•	•	•	•	•	•	All day fish market
Marseille:(02) pl de Lench	•	•	•	•	•	•		
Marseille:(02) pl Jules Guesde	•	•	•	•	•	•		
Marseille:(02) pl Sadi Carnot	•	•	•	•	•	•		Flowers
Marseille:(03) Belle-mai, pl Cadenaut	•	•	•	•	•	•		
Marseille:(03) St.Lazaire	•	•	•	•	•	•		
Marseille:(04) pl Sebastopol	•	•	•	•	•	•		
Marseille:(05) Boulevard Chav	•							Flowers
Marseille:(05) pl Jean Jaurès	•	•		•	•	•	•	
Marseille:(06) Cours Julien	•	•	•	•	•	•		Books 2nd Saturday & bric-a-brac 2nd Sunday
Marseille:(06) Cours Pierre Puget	•	•	•	•	•			
Marseille:(06) pl Félix Baret	•							Flowers
Marseille:(06) Prado, Castellane	•	•	•	•	•	•		
Marseille:(07) pl Joseph Etienne	•	•	•	•	•	•		
Marseille:(08) Bonneveine, Euromarché	•	•	•	•	•	•	•	
Marseille:(08) Pointe Rouge	•	•	•	•	•	•		
Marseille:(08) Ste Anne, Pl Bavarel	•	•	•	•	•	•		
Marseille:(09) Bd Michelet	•	•	•	•	•	•		
Marseille:(12) Caillols, Parking Sodim	•	•	•	•	•	•		All day
Marseille:(13) Métro La Rose	•	•	•	•	•	•		All day
Marseille:(14) Le canet, Place des E.U.	•	•	•	•	•	•		
Marseille:(14) Ste Marthe, P.Durand	•	•	•	•	•	•		
Marseille:(15) St-Antoine,P.Canovas	•	•	•	•	•	•		
Marseille:(15) St-Louis, Vielle Église	•	•	•	•	•			
Marseille:(16) Estaque plage					•			
Martigues: Carro	•	•	•	•	•	•	•	Fish
Martigues: Jonquières			•			•		
Martigues: Jonquières, l'Ile			•			•		
Martigues: La Couronne					•			
Martigues: Z.A.C. des Etangs						•	•	All day
Maussane: Les ALilles:pl Henri Giraud			•					
Maussane: pl Laugier d Monblan				•				
Meyrargues: av De la République							•	
Meyrargues: pl des anciens combat		•						
Meyreuil: Plan de Mayreuil		•						
Miramas: Les Molières					•			
Miramas: Miramas le Vieux		•						Tuesday afternoon
Miramas: pl Jourdan, Jean Jaurès			•					
Mollégès		•						
Mouriès: parking de l'Europe					•			
Noves: pl Jean Jaurès			•					
Orgon: pl Albert Gérard		•						
Pélissane: pl Roux de Brignoles							•	
Peynier: Cours Albéric Laurent				•				
Peypin: av De Valdonne		•						
Peyrolles: lace Albert Laurent		•			•			
Plan de Cuques					•			
Plan de Cuques: rue de 18 Juin					•			
Port de Bouc: centre ville		•	•	•	•	•	•	
Port St-Louis: centre ville			•					

Location	M	T	W	Th	F	S	Su	Comments
Puyricard: pl de l' Église					•			
Rognac: pl St.Jacques			•					
Rognes: pl du village			•					
Rognonas: pl du marché		•						
Roquefort: pl de la Poste					•			
Roquevaire: Cours Negrel Féraud					•			
Rousset: pl Paul Borde			•					
Salon de Provence: av de Wertheim		•						
Salon de Provence: pl Gl De Gaulle							•	
Salon de Provence: pl Morgan les cours			•					
Salon de Provence: quart des Bressons						•		
Salon de Provence: quart des Canourges					•			
Sausset les Pins: Le Port					•			
Senas: pl du 11 Novembre	•	•	•	•	•	•	•	
Senas: pl du la marché	•		•		•	•		Daily May to October
Septemès les Vallons: pl de la Mairie	•				•			
Simiane Collongue: cours des Héros			•		•			
St-Andiol: pl de la Mairie					•			
St-Cannat: bd Marcel Parraud			•					
St-Chamas: rue Gambetta					•			
St-Étienne du Grès	•		•		•			Friday evenings Daily in season
St-Martin de Crau: centre ville	•				•			Livestock on Mondays
St-Paul lez Durance: pl. Jean Santini		•						
St-Rémy de Provence: centre ville			•					
St-Victoret: pl des Ecoles			•				•	
Ste-Mitre les Remparts: pl de la Paix			•					
Stes-Maries de la Mer: pl des Gitans	•				•			
Suasset les Pins: Bd Audibert							•	
Tarascon: centre ville		•						
Trets: centre ville			•					
Val St-Andre: pl de la Poste	•		•		•			
Velaux: La Bastide Bertin						•		
Velaux: pl François Caire				•				
Venelles: Allées du Parc						•		
Ventabren: Aire de la Coopérative		•			•			Friday afternoon
Vitrolles: av des Salyens					•			
Vitrolles: centre urbain		•					•	
Vitrolles: Frescoule						•		
Vitrolles: Les Pinchinades			•					
Vitrolles: Village				•				

Department of Var

Location	M	T	W	Th	F	S	Su	Comments
Aups: pl Frédéric Mistral			•			•		
Bagnols en Foret			•			•		
Bandol: le Port		•						
Bargemon				•				
Belgentier: la place	•					•		
Besse sur Issole			•					
Bormes les Mimosas: Pin de Bormes		•						

Location	M	T	W	Th	F	S	Su	Comments
Bormes les Mimosas: pl St-Francois de Paule			•		•			Friday evening crafts
Brignoles: pl du 8 Mai			•			•		Saturday flowers
Brignoles: sq St-Louis					•			
Brue Auriac		•			•			
Cabasse		•			•			Tuesday smaller market than Saturday
Carcès					•			
Carqueiranne				•				
Cavalaire sur Mer			•					
Claviers		•			•			
Cogolin: pl Etienne Dolet					•			
Cogolin: pl Victor Hugo			•					
Cotignac		•						
Cuers				•				
Draguignan			•			•		Local Produce
Entrecasteaux				•				
Fayence		•		•		•		
Flayosc: pl de la République	•							
Forcalqueiret				•			•	
Fréjus: centre				•		•		
Fréjus: de St-Aygulf		•			•			
Fréjus: des Arénes						•		seasonal Saturday evenings
Fréjus: du Port				•				
Fréjus: Fréjus plage		•			•			
Fréjus: la Tour de Mare				•				
Garéoult		•						
Gonfaron				•				
Grimaud				•				
Grimaud: Port Grimaud				•			•	
Grimaud: Port Grimaud Sud	•				•			
Hyéres les Palmiers		•		•		•		Organic produce
Hyères les Palmiers: des Ille d' Or						•		
Hyères les Palmiers: pl de la République		•		•				
Hyéres les Palmiers: pl Massillon	•	•	•	•	•	•	•	Local produce
La Crau			•					
La Croix Valmer							•	
La Farlède: la place		•		•				
La Garde		•			•	•		
La Garde Freinet			•				•	
La Roquebrussanne				•	•			
La Seyne sur Mer: Louis Blanc	•	•	•	•	•	•	•	
La Seyne sur Mer: pl Lalo aux Sablettes	•	•	•	•	•	•	•	
La Valette du Var: pl de la Mairie	•							
Le Beausset: pl du village					•		•	
Le Luc					•			
Le Muy				•			•	
Le Pradet		•		•				
Les Arcs sur Argens				•			•	3rd Sunday
Les Issambres: pl de San peïre	•							
Lorgues		•						
Mazaugues		•						
Montmeyan		•			•			

Location	M	T	W	Th	F	S	Su	Comments
Nans les Pins							•	
Ollioules			•		•			
Pourrières			•					
Ramatuelle: pl de l' Ormeau			•				•	
Ravol Canadel sur Mer					•			
Régusse							•	
Rians					•			
Roquebrune sur Argens	•				•			
Salernes			•				•	
Sanary sur Mer			•					
Solliès Pont: long du boulodrome			•					
Solliès Toucas				•				
St-Cyr sur Mer: pl de Appel du 18 Juin			•			•		Local produce
St-Cyr sur Mer: Port de la Madrague	•			•				Local Produce
St-Cyr sur Mer: sq Gabriel Péri		•			•		•	
St-Mandrier sur Mer			•			•		Local produce
St-Maxim la Ste-Baume			•					
St-Raphaël			•					
St-Raphaël: Boulouris	•							
St-Raphael: centre ville				•				
St-Raphael: marché aux poissons	•	•	•	•	•	•	•	
St-Raphael: marché d' Agay			•					
St-Raphaël: pl Coullet	•			•				
St-Raphaël: pl Victor Hugo	•	•	•	•	•	•	•	
St-Tropez: halle aux poissons	•	•	•	•	•	•	•	
St-Tropez: pl des lices		•			•			
Ste-Maxime					•			
Ste-Maxime: marché couvert	•	•	•	•	•	•	•	All day in summer & mornings in winter
Ste-Maxime: vieux qrts				•				Regional produce
Toulon: Cours Lafayette	•	•	•	•	•	•	•	
Toulon: pl Dupuy de l' Home					•			Organic produce
Toulon: pl Emile Claude Mourillon	•	•	•	•	•	•	•	
Toulon: pl Martin Bidouré	•	•	•	•	•	•	•	
Toulon: pl Monseigneur Deydier Mourillon	•	•	•	•	•	•	•	
Toulon: Pont duLas	•	•	•	•	•	•	•	
Tourves		•						
Trans en Provence	•			•			•	Sunday traditional market
Varages	•			•				
Vidauban			•				•	
Villecroze				•				
Vinon sur Verdon							•	

Department of Vaucluse

Location	M	T	W	Th	F	S	Su	Comments
Apt: centre		•			•			Tuesday local produce May to November
Avignon: Jean XXIII			•					
Avignon: La Trillade		•						
Avignon: les Halles pl Pie		•	•	•	•	•	•	
Avignon: Monclar: pl J.P.Rameau		•		•				
Avignon: Montfavt		•						

Location	M	T	W	Th	F	S	Su	Comments
Avignon: pl Crillon					•			
Avignon: pl des Carmes						•		Flowers
Avignon: Pont des 2 Eaux					•			
Avignon: rempart St-Michel						•	•	Fripes
Bedarrides	•							
Bollène: pl de la Mairie	•							
Bonnieux				•				
Cadenet: centre ville	•					•		Local produce May - November
Camaret		•					•	3rd Tuesday
Caromb		•						
Carpentras		•			•			Tuesday organic produce at rue Raspail
Cavaillon: centre ville	•							
Châteauneuf du Pape				•				
Courthezon				•				
Coustellet			•				•	Local produce Wednesday evening July to August
Entraigues			•					
Gordes		•						
Grillon					•			
Isle sur la Sorgue				•			•	
Jonquières					•			
Le Pontet				•				
Le Thor		•			•			
Lourmarin				•				
Malaucène			•					
Mondragon		•						
Morieres			•					
Mormoiron							•	Local produce June to September
Orange: qrt Passadoire	•	•	•	•	•	•	•	
Pernes						•		
Pertuis			•		•	•		Local produce Wednesday & Saturday
Petit Palais					•			Local produce May to October
Sault			•					
Sorgues							•	
St-Saturnin	•							
Tour d' Aigues		•						
Vaison la Romaine		•						
Valréas			•			•		
Vedene		•						
Velleron		•				•	•	Local produce from 14.30 October to April

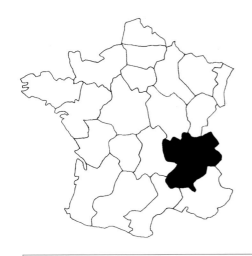

DEPARTMENTS

Ain	(1)
Ardèche	(7)
Drôme	(26)
Isère	(38)
Loire	(42)
Rhône	(69)
Savoie	(73)
Haute Savoie	(74)

Department of Ain								
Location	M	T	W	Th	F	S	Su	Comments
Ambérieu en Bugey			•			•		
Bâgé le Châtel		•						
Bellegarde sur Valserine				•				
Belley						•		1st Monday
Bourge en Bresse			•			•		
Bourge en Bresse: Champ de Foire			•			•		
Bourge en Bresse: qrt de Vennes							•	
Cerdon					•			
Chalamont: pl du marché	•							
Champagne en Valromey				•				
Châtillon sur Chalaronne						•		
Coligny		•						
Cormoz		•						
Culoz			•					
Divonne les Bains					•		•	
Dompierre sur Veyle		•						
Fareins		•						
Ferney Voltaire						•		
Foissiat						•		
Gex						•		
Hauteville Lompnes				•		•		Thursday evening
Jassans Riottier						•		
Jujurieux		•						
La Boisse			•			•		
Lagnieu: pl de l' Église	•							
Manziat				•				
Marboz	•							
Messimy sur Saône						•		
Meximieux			•					
Mézériat					•			
Miribel			•					

Location	M	T	W	Th	F	S	Su	Comments
Montluel					•			
Montmerle				•				
Montrevel		•						
Nantua						•		
Neyron					•			
Oyonnax: parc Jeautet	•					•		
Poncin	•							
Pont d'Ain						•		
Pont de Vaux				•				
Pont de Veyle: pl du marché	•							
Reyrieux		•					•	
Sault Brénaz				•				
Seyssel						•		
St-André de Corcy							•	
St-Denis en Bugey						•		
St-Didier sur Chalaronne					•			
St-Genis Pouilly					•			Friday evening
St-Jean sur Reyssouze						•		
St-Laurent sur Saône						•		
St-Maurice de Beynost						•		
St-Nizier le Bouchoux				•				
St-Paul de Varax				•				
St-Rambert en Bugey				•				
St-Trivier de Courtes	•							
Tenay					•			
Thoiry							•	
Thoissey				•				
Treffort Cuisiat					•			
Trévoux			•			•		
Villars les Dombes		•						
Villereversure						•		
Virieu le Grand		•						
Vonnas				•				

Department of Ardèche

Location	M	T	W	Th	F	S	Su	Comments
Alba la Romaine							•	
Andance					•			
Annonay: pl de la Liberté			•			•	•	Flea market & second hand fair 2nd Sunday
Antraigues			•					Evening October to December
Arlebosc	•	•	•	•	•	•	•	Sunday June & July
Aubenas: centre					•			
Baix			•					
Bourg St-Andéol			•			•		Flea market 1st Saturday
Burzet			•				•	
Charmes sur Rhône					•			
Chomérac				•				
Coucouron			•					
Cruas					•			
Davézieux					•			Evening

Location	M	T	W	Th	F	S	Su	Comments
Désaignes	•	•	•	•	•	•	•	Evening June
Guilherand				•				
Jaujac: pl du Champ de Mars		•		•				
Joyeuse			•					
La Voulte sur Rhône				•			•	4th Sunday
Labégude				•				
Lablachère							•	
Lalevade		•						
Lalouvesc			•					
Lamastre: pl Seignobos		•						
Largentière: pl des Recollets		•						
Lavilledieu			•					
Le Cheylard			•					
Le Lac d'Issarlès			•				•	seasonal
Le Pouzin			•					
Le Teil			•					
Les Vans					•			
Mauves	•	•	•	•	•	•	•	seasonal
Meyras Neyrac les Bains			•					
Meysse							•	
Montpezat sous Bauzon				•				
Privas			•			•	•	Flea market 2nd Sunday
Rochemaure		•						
Rosières: av André Jean	•							
Ruoms					•			
Sarras			•					
Satillieu		•						
Serrières					•			
Soyons			•					
St-Agrève	•							June to August
St-Cirgues en Montagne							•	
St-Félicien					•			
St-Jean de Muzols			•					
St-Martin d'Ardèche							•	
St-Martind de Valamas			•					
St-Paul le Jeune	•				•			
St-Péray			•					
St-Pierre de Colombier	•	•	•	•	•	•	•	seasonal
St-Pierreville							•	seasonal
St-Sauveur de Montagut					•			
Thueyts					•			
Tournon sur Rhône			•			•		
Valgorge							•	
Vallon Pont d'Arc				•				
Vals les Bains							•	
Vernoux				•				
Villeneuve de Berg			•					
Viviers		•						
Vogüé	•							

Department of Drôme

Location	M	T	W	Th	F	S	Su	Comments
Allex	•							
Anneyron		•						
Aouste sur Sye						•		Evening
Beaufort sur Gervanne			•				•	Sunday seasonal
Beaumont lès Valence						•		
Bourdeaux				•				
Buis les Baronnies			•			•		
Chabeuil: qui de République		•						
Chamaret				•				
Châteauneuf de Galaure			•					
Châtillon en Diois				•				
Clavyson	•		•	•				
Cléon d'Andran		•						
Clerieux						•		
Crest		•				•		Friday evening
Die			•			•		
Dieulefit				•				
Donzère						•		
Érôme			•					
Étoile sur Rhône			•					
Grâne				•				
Grignan		•						
Hauterives		•						
La Bégude de Mazenc		•						
La Chapelle en Vercors			•			•		Saturday seasonal
La Motte Chalancon	•							July - August
La Roche de Glun			•					
Le Grand Serre					•			
Les Granges Gontardes			•					
Livron sur Drôme		•				•		
Loriol sur Drôme	•				•			
Luc en Diois					•			
Lus la Croix Haute			•					
Malissard			•					
Marsanne					•			
Mirabel aux Barronnies					•			
Montbrun les Bains						•		
Montélimar: centre		•				•		
Montélimar: St-James				•				
Montmeyran		•						
Montségur Lauzon			•					
Nyons			•				•	Sunday seasonal
Peyrins			•					
Pierrelatte				•				
Pont de Barret				•				
Rémuzat			•					
Rochegude				•				
Romans: pl Maurice Faure	•	•			•	•	•	
Saillans							•	

Location	M	T	W	Th	F	S	Su	Comments
Salles sous Bois		•						
Saon					•			
Saulce sur Rhône				•				
Sauzet					•			
Sederon							•	seasonal
St-Donat sur l'Herbasse	•							
St-Gervais sur Roubion		•						
St-Jean en Royans				•		•		Saturday evening seasonal & 2nd Monday
St-Laurent en Royans				•				
St-Nazaire en Royans			•					
St-Paul Trois Châteaux		•						
St-Rambert d'Albon					•			
St-Uze							•	
St-Vallier				•				
Suze la Rousse					•			
Tain l'Hermitage					•			
Taulignan					•			
Tulette	•							
Valaurie							•	seasonal
Valence: av Georges Clemenceau					•			
Valence: bd Bancel			•					
Valence: pl Danton	•							
Valence: pl de l'Europe		•				•		
Valence: pl de la Dragonne						•		Organic food
Valence: pl de la Paix			•					
Valence: pl des Clercs				•		•		
Valence: pl Jean Perrin				•				
Valence: pl Lamartine					•			
Valence: pl St-Jean		•						
Valence: Pont des Anglais	•	•				•		Large afternoon markets until 15.00hrs
Valence: rue Jules Ferry			•					
Valence: rue Malossane		•						
Valence: rue Marx Dormoy				•				

Department of Isère

Location	M	T	W	Th	F	S	Su	Comments
Allevard				•				
Autrans: centre			•					
Beaurepaire: pl de la Paix			•					
Bourg d'Oisans: Parking du Musée						•		rue de Viennois et du General D Gaulle in summer
Bourgoin Jallieu: Champfleuri			•					
Bourgoin Jallieu: pl Carnot et G.de Gaulle				•			•	
Bourgoin Jallieu: pl Théodore Diederichs						•		Saturday afternoon
Brié et Angonnes: av Mail à Tavrnolles		•						Tuesday afternoon
Brignoud		•				•		
Cessieu	•							
Charavines							•	
Chasse sur Rhône		•		•				
Crémieu			•					

Location	M	T	W	Th	F	S	Su	Comments
Crolles: pl de la Mairie							•	
Crolles: pl de la Mairie			•					
Domène			•					
Échirolles			•	•	•		•	
Eybens		•						
Fontaine: Marcel Cachin		•		•		•	•	
Fontaine: Péri			•		•			
Gières			•					
Grenoble: de l'Abbaye		•					•	
Grenoble: Estacade		•	•	•	•	•	•	
Grenoble: Halles St-Claire		•	•	•	•	•	•	Friday & Saturday all day
Grenoble: Hébert		•		•	•		•	
Grenoble: Hoche					•			
Grenoble: Les Eaux Claires					•			
Grenoble: Malherbe		•	•	•	•	•	•	
Grenoble: marché Liberation		•			•	•		
Grenoble: Mistral					•	•		
Grenoble: pl des Herbes		•	•	•	•	•	•	
Grenoble: pl Ste-Claire		•	•	•	•	•	•	
Grenoble: St-André		•	•	•	•	•	•	
Grenoble: St-Bruno		•	•	•	•	•	•	
Grenoble: Victor Hugo	•	•	•	•	•	•	•	
Grenoble: Villeneuve		•	•	•	•	•	•	
Heyrieux					•			
Izeaux					•			
L' Isle d'Abeau			•		•			
La Côte St-André			•					
La Mûre d'Isere: parkings	•							
La Tour du Pin: pl Carnot		•			•			
La Tronche: rue de l'Isère					•			
La Verpillière: pl J.Serlin		•					•	
Lancey					•			
Lans en Vercors		•						
Le Champ près Froges				•				
Le Grand Lemps: pl du Chateau		•		•				
Le Péage de Roussillon			•		•			
Le Pont de Beauvoisin: centre ville	•							
Les Abrets			•					
Meylan		•	•	•	•	•	•	
Moirans					•			
Montalieu Vercieu					•			
Montbonnot St-Martin				•				
Morestel: pl des Halles et du 8 mai 1945							•	
Pont de Chéruy							•	
Pont de Claix: pl du Marché							•	
Pont en Royans: pl de la Mairie			•					
Pontcharra			•					
Rives: pl Xavier Brochier			•			•		Saturday afternoon
Roussillon: pl de la République			•				•	
Sassenage: pl de l'Europe					•			
Seyssinet Pariset		•		•		•		

Location	M	T	W	Th	F	S	Su	Comments
St-André le Gaz							●	
St-Antoine l'Abbaye				●				
St-Egrève: rue des Bonnais					●			Friday afternoon
St-Egrève: Square Armand Nordon		●			●			
St-Étienne de St-Geoirs: pl Alexandrine Gagneux	●							
St-Georges d'Espéranche			●					
St-Ismier					●			
St-Jean de Bournay: pl du marché	●							
St-Laurent du Pont: av G.de.Gaulle			●					
St-Marcellin: pl du Kiosque		●			●	●		
St-Martin d'Uriage			●					
St-Martin le Vinoux: pl Pasteur				●				
St-Pierre de Chartreuse: au Plan de Ville					●			
Uriage les Bains	●							seasonal
Varces						●		
Vienne: Estressin		●	●		●	●		
Vif: pl de la Mairie					●			
Villard de Lans			●				●	
Villefontaine			●		●			
Vinay: Parking du Dr.Dupré	●							
Vizille: pl du Marché		●						
Voiron: pl G.de Gaulle			●		●			
Voreppe: pl Armand Pugnot					●			

Department of Loire

Location	M	T	W	Th	F	S	Su	Comments
Andrèzieux Bouthèon: Bouthéon				●				
Andrèzieux Bouthèon: La Chapelle				●				Afternoon
Andrèzieux Bouthèon: Le Bourg		●						
Bonson: place du 11 Novembre							●	
Cellieu	●	●	●	●	●	●	●	Every afternoon Cherries May to July.
Chazelles sur Lyon: pl Poterne		●	●					
Farnay				●				Thursday afternoon
Firminy: pl du Breuil				●				All day
Firminy: pl du Marché		●		●		●		
Fraisses: pl Jean Rist		●						
Génilac				●				
L' Etrat: pl du Plâtre			●				●	Wednesday afternoon
L' Horme: Cours Marin			●					
La Fouillouse: pl de l' Église					●			
La Grand Croix: pl C. de Gaulle	●							
La Ricamarie: pl Michel Rondet et Raspail			●			●		
La Talaudière: pl de la Mairie		●				●		
Le Chambon Feugerolles : pl de l'église						●		
Le Chambon Feugerolles : pl de la Romière							●	
Le Chambon Feugerolles : pl J.Jaurès			●					
Le Chambon Feugerolles : pl J.Jaurès et Halles	●					●		
Lorette: pl Rivoire Villemange							●	
Rive de Gier: Au Grand Point			●					
Rive de Gier: pl de la Libération		●				●		

Location	M	T	W	Th	F	S	Su	Comments
Roche la Moliere: Beaulieu pl du Borugeat		•			•			
Roche la Molière: pl Jean Jaurès			•		•			
Sorbiers: pl du 8 Mai 1945					•			
St-Chamond: pl de Bonnevialle	•							
St-Chamond: pl de la Liberté		•		•	•			
St-Chamond: pl Louis Comte et elle de France				•	•			
St-Chamond: pl Nationale et Neyrand					•			
St-Chamond: pl St-Pierre				•	•			Friday afternoon
St-Etienne: Côte Chaude				•	•			
St-Etienne: Cours Fauriel				•	•			
St-Etienne: Crêt de Roc				•				
St-Etienne: Fourneyron		•			•	•		
St-Etienne: La Cotonne				•	•			
St-Etienne: La Dame Blanche				c				
St-Etienne: La Métare					•			
St-Etienne: La Rivière		•			•			
St-Etienne: La Terrasse pl Massenet				•	•			
St-Etienne: Montchovet				•			•	
St-Etienne: Monthieu				•				
St-Etienne: Montplaisir		•		•				
St-Etienne: Montreynaud			•	•				
St-Etienne: pl Albert Thomas		•		•	•			
St-Etienne: pl Bellevue		•		•			•	
St-Etienne: pl Boivin	•	•	•	•	•	•	•	
St-Etienne: pl Carnot		•			•		•	
St-Etienne: pl Garibaldi	•			•				
St-Etienne: pl Grenette					•			
St-Etienne: pl Jacquard	•			•	•	•		
St-Etienne: pl Jules Ferry				•	•			
St-Etienne: rue Léon Nautin		•		•	•			
St-Etienne: Solaure		•		•				
St-Etienne: square Massenet			•					
St-Etienne: St-François			•				•	
St-Etienne: St.Roch		•		•	•			
St-Etienne: Terrenoire			•					
St-Galmier: pl de la Devise	•							
St-Genest Lerpt: pl Carnot				•	•			
St-Just St-Rambert: pl de la République				•			•	
St-Just St-Rambert: pl du Marché				•	•			
St-Marcellin en Forez: rue A.Briand							•	
St-Paul en Jarez: pl Lisfranc				•			•	
St-Priest en Jarez		•						
Sury le Comtal			•					
Unieux: Côte Quart Sempico		•						
Unieux: Val Ronzière		•						
Veauche: pl Aristide Briand			•		•			
Veauche: pl J.Raffin					•			
Vllars: pl Gambetta				•				

Department of Rhône								
Location	M	T	W	Th	F	S	Su	Comments
Alix: pl Mairie					•			Afternoon
Amplepuis: rue Hôtel de Ville		•						
Ampuis: pl des Anciens Combattants			•					
Anse: av de Brianne					•			
Arnas: parking du Bourg				•				
Bagnols: pl de la Mairie					•			Afternoon
Beaujeu: pl Hôtel de Ville			•					
Belleville sur Saône: pl du Marché		•						
Bessenay: pl du Marché				•				
Bois d'Oingt: pl de la Libération		•						
Bourg de Thizy: pl République							•	
Brignais: pl du 8 Mai 1945					•			
Brindas: pl de Verdun					•			
Bron: av du 8 Mai 1945				•				
Bron: pl de l'Eglise			•					
Bron: pl de la Liberté	•				•			
Bron: pl Jean Moulin		•				•		
Bron: rue Louis Blanc				•				
Bron: sq Laurent Bonnevay							•	
Brullioles: pl Neuve					•			Afternoon 15.30 to 19.00
Brussieu: pl de Mairie					•			
Bully: pl de l'Eglise			•		•			
Cailloux sur Fontaines: plde la Mairie					•			
Caluire et Cuire: allée de la Jeunesse				•	•			
Caluire et Cuire: pl des Moulins du Rhône		•						
Chambost Longessaigne: pl de l'Eglise				•	•			
Champagne au Mt d'Or: pl Ludovic Monnier				•				
Chaponnay: pl de la Mairie				•				
Chaponost: pl du 8 Mai 1945							•	
Charbonnieres les Bains: pl St-Luce				•				
Charly: parking de la Poste				•				
Chassagny: pl St-Roc		•						
Chasselay: rue Bellecize				•				
Chassieu: pl Jean-Fleury Coponat			•		•			
Chatillon d' Azergues: pl de la Mairie					•			
Chaussan: pl de l'Eglise					•			Afternoon 16.30 to 18.30
Chazay d' Azergues: pl de la Platière				•				
Chessy les Mines: pl de la Mairie					•			
Collonges au Mt d'Or: pl du Général de Gaulle				•				
Communay: pl du Marché			•					
Condrieu: pl du Marché					•			
Corbas: av des Frères Lumière						•		
Corbas: pl de la Mairie					•			
Cours la Ville: pl de l'Eglise			•		•			
Cours la Ville: pl de la Mairie	•		•		•			
Cours la Ville: pl de la République	•							
Cours la Ville: rue Centrale	•							
Courzieu: pl de la Mairie			•				•	
Couzon au Mt d'Or: pl de la Liberté							•	

Location	M	T	W	Th	F	S	Su	Comments
Craponne: pl Andrée Marie Perrin						•		
Craponne: rue Centrale			•					
Decines Charpieu: pl de la Libération				•				
Decines Charpieu: pl Henri Barbusse							•	
Decines Charpieu: pl Mendès-France					•			
Decines Charpieu: pl Roger Salengro		•						
Ecully: pl du Marché				•	•			
Feyzin: pl Claudius Bery				•				Afternoon
Fleurie: pl de l'Eglise					•			
Fleurieu sur Saône: pl de la Mairie			•					
Fontaine sur Saône: pl de l'Eglise			•					
Fontaine sur Saône: qrt des Marronniers				•				
Francheville: pl de la Poste				•				
Francheville: rue du Robert			•					
Frontenas: Pl des 3 Platanes							•	
Genas: pl Ronshausen							•	
Genay: pl Verdun					•			
Givors: av du Maréchal Leclerc		•						
Givors: pl du Général de Gaulle			•					
Givors: pl Henri Barbusse			•				•	
Givors: pl Jean Jaurès			•		•		•	
Givors: qrt de Vernes			•					
Grandris: Nouvelle place			•					
Grezieu la Varenne: Halle municipal		•						
Grigny: pl Jean Jaurès			•					Afternoon
Haute Rivoire: pl du Monument aux Morts			•					Afternoon
Irigny: pl de l'Europe			•		•			
Jonage: pl de Général de Gaulle			•				•	
Julienas: pl du Marché	•							
L' Arbresle: pl République				•				
La Mulatiere: pl Jean Moulin		•		•				
Lacenas: pl du Marché			•					
Lamure sur Azergues: av de la Gare					•			
Lentilly: pl de l'Eglise			•					
Limas: rue Pierre Ponot		•				•	•	
Limonest: pl Décurel			•					
Limonest: pl Griffon					•			
Lissieu: Bois Dieu		•						Afternoon 15.00 to 19.00
Lissieu: Bourg					•			Afternoon 15.00 to 19.00
Loire sur Rhône: pl de la Poste		•						
Longessaigne: pl de l'Eglise			•					Afternoon 15.00 to 19.00
Lozanne: pl du Marché			•		•			Organic produce Saturday afternoon
Lucenay: pl de l'Eglise			•					
Lyon(1): bd Croix Rousse		•	•	•	•	•	•	
Lyon(2): cours Bayard			•				•	
Lyon(2): pl Carnot							•	Also pets
Lyon(2): quai St-Antoine		•	•	•	•	•	•	
Lyon(3): Montchat			•		•			
Lyon(3): pl des Martyrs			•					
Lyon(3): pl Guichard		•					•	
Lyon(3): quai Victor Augagneur		•	•	•	•	•	•	

Location	M	T	W	Th	F	S	Su	Comments
Lyon(3): rue Bellacombe		•						
Lyon(3): rue Gabillot			•		•			
Lyon(4): Camille Flamarion			•		•			
Lyon(4): petite pl de la Croix Rousse		•	•	•	•	•	•	
Lyon(4): pl du Commandant Arnaud				•				
Lyon(5): av Buyer					•			
Lyon(5): bd des Castors							•	
Lyon(5): Ménival			•				•	
Lyon(5): pl Bénédict-Tessier		•		•				
Lyon(5): rue César Geoffrey		•						
Lyon(5): rue des Anges		•			•			
Lyon(5): St-Jean pl Conette				•				Organic produce
Lyon(6): rue Boileau Mongolfier			•					
Lyon(7): av Jean Jaurès		•		•			•	
Lyon(7): Brotteaux			•		•			
Lyon(7): pl Jean Macé			•		•			
Lyon(7): pl St-Louis		•		•			•	
Lyon(8): Etats-Unis pl du 8 Mai 1945		•	•		•			
Lyon(8): pl Ambroise Courtois		•	•		•			
Lyon(8): pl Ambroise Paré			•				•	
Lyon(8): pl Belleville			•				•	
Lyon(8): pl du Général André							•	
Lyon(8): rue de Narvick					•			
Lyon(8): rue Joseph Challier					•			
Lyon(9): Duchère Balmont					•			
Lyon(9): Duchère Sauvegarde			•				•	
Lyon(9): pl Vanderpol		•						Organic produce
Lyon(9): Plateau Duchère				•				
Lyon(9): qtr Vergoin		•						
Lyon(9): quai Sédaillan				•				
Lyon(9): rue Jean Zai		•		•				
Lyon(9): rue Roger Salengro			•			•	•	
Marennes: pl de l'Eglise		•						Afternoon 16.00 to 20.00
Marennes: pl du Champ de Mars				•				
Messimy: pl de l'Eglise				•				Afternoon 16.00 to 20.00
Meyzieu: pl des Droits de l'Homme	•							
Meyzieu: pl Jean Monet			•		•			
Millery: pl de la Mairie				•	•			
Mions: rue du 19 Mars 1962			•		•			
Monsols: pl de la Fontaine							•	2nd & 4th Saturday
Montagny: pl de la Mairie		•						
Montrottier: pl du Centre		•						Afternoon
Mornant: pl de la Liberté					•			
Neuville sur Saône: pl du Marché					•			
Oingt: pl de Presberg					•			
Orlienas: pl François Blanc				•				
Oullins: Cite Ampère					•			
Oullins: parking Kellerman							•	
Oullins: pl Anatole France		•	•					
Oullins: pl Labussière					•			
Oullins: rue Pierre Sémard				•				Afternoon

Location	M	T	W	Th	F	S	Su	Comments
Perreon: au Bourg				•				
Pierre Benite: pl de la Paix		•					•	
Pollionnay: pl des Platanes		•						
Pommiers: centre comm de Trézette					•			
Pontcharra sur Turdine: pl de l'Eglise				•				Afternoon
Pusignan: pl de la Valla				•				
Quincieux: pl de l'Eglise				•				Afternoon
Regnie Durette: pl de l'Eglise			•					Afternoon 13.30 to 17.30
Rillieux la Pape: Alagniers		•					•	
Rillieux la Pape: pl Canelasse					•			
Rillieux la Pape: pl Maréchal Juin				•				
Rillieux la Pape: qrt de la Roue					•			
Sain Bel: pl du Marché					•			
Sathonay Camp: av Pérouges		•						
Sathonay Village: pl L. Danis					•			
Solaize: pl de la Mairie							•	
Soucieu en Jarrest: pl de la Flette		•						
St-Bonnet de Mure: pl del'ancienne Mairie			•					
St-Clement les Places: Le Bourg					•			Afternoon
St-Cyr au Mt d'Or: pl de la République					•			
St-Didier au Mt d'Or: pl André Michel		•						
St-Etienne des Oullieres: pl de la Mairie		•						
St-Fons: pl Durel		•			•			
St-Genis Laval: pl de la Mairie			•					
St-Genis Laval: pl Jaboulay		•		•				
St-Genis Laval: rue de la République			•					Organic produce
St-Genis les Ollieres: pl de la Mairie			•					
St-Genis les Ollieres: pl George Pompidou							•	
St-Georges de Reneins: pl de l'Eglise					•			
St-Igny de Vers: la place		•						
St-Laurent d'Argny: pl Neuve		•			•			Afternoon
St-Laurent d'Oingt: salle des Fêtes			•					
St-Laurent de Chamousset: pl du Marché	•							
St-Laurent de Mure: pl Honoré de Balzac	•	•			•			Friday Afternoon
St-Martin en Haut: pl de l'Eglise	•				•			Monday afternoon 11.00 to 17.00
St-Pierre de Chandieu: la place					•			
St-Pierre la Palud: pl de l'Eglise			•					
St-Priest: pl Ferdinand Buisson				•				
St-Priest: pl Roger Salengro		•					•	
St-Priest: qrt Diderot					•			
St-Priest: rue Louis Braille			•					
St-Symphorien d'Ozon: pl du Docteur Cinelli				•				
St-Symphorien sur Coise: pl du Marchê		•						All day also at pl de Verdun & pl Mezel
Ste-Colombine: pl Aristide Briand		•						Organic produce
Ste-Concorce: pl de l'Eglise							•	
Ste-Foy l'Argentiere: pl du Centre			•					Also pl du Château & pl de la Gare
Ste-Foy les Lyon: bd des Provinces		•			•			
Ste-Foy les Lyon: pl Choubeyrat		•			•			
Ste-Foy les Lyon: pl François Millou			•					
Ste-Foy les Lyon: rue Laurent Paul			•					
Ste-Paule: pl Publique			•					

Location	M	T	W	Th	F	S	Su	Comments
Taluyers: pl de la Bascule			•		•			
Tarare: marchê couvert				•	•			
Tarare: pl Janisson				•	•			
Tassin la Demi Lune: pl de Tassin			•					
Tassin la Demi Lune: pl Peraguit								
Ternay: pl de l'Eglise	•				•			
Thizy: pl de l'Eglise					•			
Thizy: pl de la Rêpublique			•					
Thurins: pl Dugas				•				
Tour de Salvagny: pl de la Mairie				•				
Toussieu: pl de la Mairie					•			
Vaugneray: pl du Marché		•			•			
Vaulx en Velin: av Georges Dimitrov				•				
Vaulx en Velin: av Roger Salengro			•		•			
Vaulx en Velin: pl du Marché					•			
Vaulx en Velin: pl François Mauriac			•		•			
Vaulx en Velin: pl Gilbert Boissier	•							
Venissieux: aux Minguettes				•	•			
Venissieux: Charréard					•			
Venissieux: Parilly					•			
Venissieux: pl du Moulin à Vent				•				
Venissieux: pl Léon Sublet			•				•	
Vernaison: pl du 11 Novembre			•		•			
Ville sur Jarnioux: la Place					•			Afternoon 17.00 to 18.00
Villecheneve: pl de la Bascule			•					
Villefranche sur Saône: Beligny					•			
Villefranche sur Saône: Belleroche		•			•			
Villefranche sur Saône: marché couvert	•				•			
Villefranche sur Sôane: pl 11 Nov.	•						•	
Villefranche sur Sôane: pl Claude Bernard			•				•	
Villeurbanne: av Général Leclerc				•			•	
Villeurbanne: av Roberto Rossellini	•							Afternoon
Villeurbanne: av St-Exupéry			•		•			
Villeurbanne: Charpenne							•	
Villeurbanne: Cité St-Jean		•	•					Tueasday afternoon
Villeurbanne: pl Chanoine Boursier		•	•		•			
Villeurbanne: pl Croix-Luizet			•		•			
Villeurbanne: pl de la Paix		•			•			
Villeurbanne: pl des Passementiers			•					
Villeurbanne: pl Grandclément		•	•				•	
Villeurbanne: pl Victor Balland			•			•		
Villeurbanne: pl Wilson			•		•		•	
Villeurbanne: rue Pierre-Joseph Proudhon				•				
Villie Morgon: pl Principale			•					
Yzeron: parking route de St-Martin en Haut							•	

Department of Savoie

Location	M	T	W	Th	F	S	Su	Comments
Aiguebelle: pl du Marché		•						
Aigueblanche					•			
Aime			•					
Aix les Bains: pl Demenceau			•		•			
Albens				•				
Albertville: pl Borrel				•	•			Thursday allday
Aussois		•						
Beaufort			•					
Bessans	•							
Bourg St-Maurice					•			
Bozel			•					
Brides les Bains			•					
Challes les Eaux		•		•				
Chambéry: centre					•			
Chambéry: le Biollay			•					
Chambéry: le Haut				•			•	
Chambéry: les halles		•	•	•	•	•		
Champagny en Vanoise		•						
Crest Voland				•				
Flumet		•						
Fontcouverte la Toussuire				•				
Fourneaux			•					
La Bathie					•			
La Chambre				•				
La Lechere	•							March to November
La Motte Servolex		•						
La Ravoire			•	•				
La Rochette			•					
Lanslebourg Mont Cenis			•					Afternoon
Lanslevillard			•					
Le Bourget du Lac			•					
Le Châtelard				•				seasonal
Lepin le Lac						•		Afternoon July to August
Les Allues		•		•				
Les Avanchers Valmorel	•			•				All day in season
Les Échelles			•					
Lescheraines: pont de Lescheraines			•					seasonal
Modane				•				
Montmélian	•							
Montvalezan		•		•		•		Saturday in summer & Tuesday in winter
Moûtiers		•			•			
Notre Dame de Bellecombe	•							seasonal
Novalaise			•				•	
Peisey Nancroix	•							Except in winter
Seez				•				Afternoon July to August
St-Bon Tarentaise			•	•				Afternoons
St-Colombans des Villards	•							1st Monday from May to September
St-Francois Longchamp						•		
St-Genix sur Guiers			•					

Location	M	T	W	Th	F	S	Su	Comments
St-Jean de Maurienne						●		
St-Martin de Belleville: Menuires			●		●			seasonal
St-Martin de Belleville: Val Thorens		●		●				
St-Michel de Maurienne					●			
St-Pierre d' Albigny			●					
St-Remy de Maurienne		●						
Termignon		●						All day
Tignes				●			●	seasonal
Val d' Isère	●							seasonal
Valloire					●			
Yenne		●						1st Tuesday

Department of Haute Savoie

Location	M	T	W	Th	F	S	Su	Comments
Abondance							●	
Ambilly					●			
Annecy: bd Taine					●			
Annecy: les Romains		●						
Annecy: Novel			●					
Annecy: Vieux qrts		●					●	
AnnemasseL pl de la Libération		●		●				
Bellegarde			●					
Boëge		●						
Bonne sur Menoge				●				
Bonneville		●		●				
Bons en Chablais					●			
Carroz d'Arâches		●						
Chamonix					●			
Châtel			●					
Chedde		●						
Cluses Sardagne			●					Afternoon
Cluses: centre ville	●							
Collonges sous Salève							●	
Combloux			●					
Cran Gevrier			●				●	
Cruseilles			●					
Doussard	●							
Douvaine							●	
Évian		●						
Evian les Bains					●			
Excenevex			●					
Favrges			●					
Frangy			●					
Gaillard					●			
Groisy		●						
La Balme de Sillingy							●	
La Chapelle d'Abondance				●				
La Clusaz: centre	●							
La Roche sur Foron			●					
Le Fayet			●					

Location	M	T	W	Th	F	S	Su	Comments
Le Grand Bornand			•					
Les Contamines Montjoie		•						
Les Gets				•				
Les Houches	•							seasonal
Marignier					•			Afternoon
Megève					•			
Meythet			•					
Mieussy						•		
Morzine			•					
Plateau d'Assy			•					
Praz sur Arly			•					
Reignier						•		
Rumilly				•				
Sallanches						•		
Samoëns			•					
Sciez						•		
Scionzier						•		
Seynod			•					
Seyssel	•							
St-Gervais				•				
St-Jean de Sixt							•	
St-Jean de Tholome						•		
St-Jeoire					•			
St-Julien en Genevois					•			
St-Pierre en Faucigny						•		
Taninges				•				
Thoiry							•	
Thônes						•		
Thonon les Bains	•			•				
Valleiry							•	
Veigy Foncenex					•			
Ville la Grand							•	
Viuz en Sallaz	•							
Vuantoine							•	

INDEX

INDEX

INDEX

INDEX

C

INDEX

INDEX

INDEX

D

INDEX

INDEX

INDEX

INDEX

INDEX

INDEX

INDEX

INDEX

INDEX

INDEX

INDEX

INDEX

INDEX

INDEX

INDEX

INDEX

INDEX

INDEX

INDEX

INDEX

INDEX

INDEX

Acknowledgements

My very good friend Liz for her encouragement

"Dick" Whittington for help with translation

The Office de Tourism in the following areas including, where known, the individual helper

Estelle at **Gap**: Caroline at **Carcassonne**: Foix: **Troyes: Aubenas**:

Jackie BRU at **Rodez** : Geraldine COURAGE at **Evreux** : **St-Brieuc** :

Caroline at **Angouleme** : Ghislaine VIOLLET at **Bourge en Bresse** : **Laon** :

Aix-en-Provence : Isabelle Nouteau at **Nantes** : Phillipe Guorand at **La Rochelle** :

Auch : **Guëret** : **St-Etienne** : **Tours** : **Cahors** : **Bordeaux** : **Valence** :

Agen : D.ANDRE at **Nimes** : **Le Puy en Velay** : **Tulle** : **Chartres** : **Orleans** :

Alain BAIGNEAU at **Toulouse** : **Bourges** : **Aurillac** : **Grenoble** : Stephanie at **Blois** :

P.TRANCHER at **Mende** : **Bergerac** : **Cherbourg** : **Brest** : Vanessa at **Nancy** :

Clermont Ferrand : **Poitiers** : **Montaubin** : **Strasbourg** : **Epinal** : Catherine at **Le Mans** :

Michel LALANNE at **Mont de Marsan** : **Belfort** : **Lille** : **Laval** : **Limoges**:

Alencon : **Lons le Saunier** : Sophie de CHASSEY at **Versailles** : **St-Dizier** :

Strasbourg : **Lorient** : **Tarbes** : **Reims** : **Perpignan** : Alexandra BODET at **Niort** :

Annecy : Irène Pecusseau at **Angers** : **Albi** : **Mâcon** : Bernadette Beaucamp at **Bihorel** :

Virginie at **Amiens** : **Bar le Duc** : Marie-France EHRET at **Mulhouse** :

Sabine BENEZET at **Avignon** : **Nevers** : **Colmar** : S.FOUCUAIT at **Montpellier** :

Pierre TRUCHI at **Pau** : **Auxerre** : **La Roche sur Yon** : Fabienne Fertilati at **Nice** :

Bobigny : **Beauvaisis** : **Chaumont** : Marion Humbaire at **Vesoul** : **Melun** : **Evry** : **Caen** :

Digne les Bains : **Arras** : Claudie CAROFF at **Nanterre** : **Strasbourg** : **Doubs** :

Hauts de Seine : Alexa at **Épernay** : Yvette EBEL **at Dormans** : **Ste-Menehould** :

Esternay

Agence Touristique at **Chambéry**

Conseil Général at **Draguignan**

Chambre de Commerce et D'Industrie : Isabelle GALLE at **Chateauroux** : **Le Mans**

Nancy : **Lyon**

Federation Nationale des Syndicats de Commercants Non Sedentaires at **Paris**

Prefecture de Moselle at **Metz**

R.VIGOT at Syndicat des Commerçants non Sédentaires de **Besançon**

Notes

I have found new markets at:

Place	Days of Week	Comments

Look out for the next books in the series

Fairs
of
France

Mussels, Mushrooms, Chestnuts, Wine, Cheese,
Books, Antiques, Bric-a-Brac, Crafts,
Merry-go-Rounds.

You will find them all in this book.

Make your holiday a time to remember
Visit a fair and pick up a memento of your stay

On Sale Soon

for advance notice of publication
please take a moment to photocopy or cut out and fill in
the page at the end of this book
or e-mail the publishers at
loisirspublications.com

Look out for the next books in the series

Festivals
of
France

Giants, Medieval Jousts, Water Battles, Donkey Derbys, Goat Races, Black Pudding Contests, Music Festivals, Art Celebrations, Fantastic Son et Lumière

You will find them all in this book.

Join in and enjoy the local celebrations.
You will be made very welcome.

On sale soon

for advance notice of publication
please take a moment to photocopy or cut out and fill in
the page at the end of this book
or e-mail the publishers at
loisirspublications.com

Notice to the Publishers

I would like to be kept informed of any further publications
on a **priority** basis and especially any
Discounts or Special Offers

My details are;

Title............Initials...........Surname...

House name or number...
First line of address..
Second line of address..
Town...
County..
Postcode...

Telephone No................................Fax No..

e-mail address...

send to or e-mail to: The Advance Subscriptions Manager,
Loisirs Publications,
Loisirs House,
27, Eagle Road,
Bishops Green,
Newbury, Berks..
RG20 4HP

e-mail loisirspublications.com